Pray & Play Bible for Young Children

Group
Loveland, Colorado

Pray & Play Bible for Young Children

Credits

Contributing Authors: Jennifer Root Wilger, Lois Keffer, Jennifer Nystrom, Bonnie Temple, Beth Rowland Wolf, Susan L. Lingo, Melissa C. Downey, and Jody Brolsma

Book Acquisitions Editor: Susan L. Lingo
Editor: Jody Brolsma
Chief Creative Officer: Joani Schultz
Copy Editor: Janis Sampson
Art Director: Lisa Chandler
Cover Art Director: Helen H. Lannis
Computer Graphic Artist: Kari K. Monson
Cover Designer: Liz Howe
Cover Illustrator: Ray Tollison
Illustrators: Mas Miyamoto (*God Made Our World*), Drew Rose (*Noah*), Vlasta Van Kampen (*Abraham*), Stacey Lamb (*Moses*), Marilyn Mets (*Samuel*), Michelle Berg (*Esther*), Pat Girouard (*Jonah*), Alan Eitzen (*Jesus' Birth*), Julie Durell (*The Little Lost Sheep*), Benrei Huang (*Jesus' Miracles*), Jennifer Schneider (*The Miracle of Easter*), Paige Billin-Frye (*Jesus Appears to His Followers*), Elizabeth Wolf (*Saul's Surprise: On the Road to Damascus*), and Rusty Fletcher (*Paul and Silas Go to Jail*)
Activity pages: Shelley Dieterichs, Bonnie Matthews, and Rebecca Thornburgh
Song pages: Ray Tollison
Production Manager: Ann Marie Gordon

Library of Congress Cataloging-in-Publication Data
Pray & play Bible for young children.
      p.   cm.
    Summary: Contains fourteen Bible stories, plus creative prayers, playtime activities, and songs to accompany each story.
    ISBN 0-7644-2024-0
    1. Bible stories, English. 2. Children--Religious life.
[1. Bible stories. 2. Christian life.] I. Group Publishing.
BS551.2.P72 1997
220.9'505--dc21   96-40288
                         CIP
                         AC

7 6 5 4 3 2   03 02 01 00 99 98 97
Printed in Hong Kong.

Stacey Kay
1675 Garnet Ave.
San Diego, CA 92109-3117

Contents

The Pray & Play Bible for Young Children will help your kids fall in love with God's Word!

"Those who love your teachings will find true peace, and nothing will defeat them" (Psalm 119:165).

There's no greater joy than seeing a child fall in love with God's Word. Excited cries of "Read it again!" "This is my favorite story!" and "Let *me* tell it this time!" bring delight to the hearts of Christian parents and teachers. But helping children develop that love and understanding of the Bible can be a challenge. Often we think Bible truths are too difficult for young children to grasp, or we're not sure how to make the Bible relevant to everyday living. And sometimes family Bible study seems downright impossible with wiggly, fidgety children!

The *Pray & Play Bible for Young Children* brings God's Word to life for little ones. These fourteen favorite Bible stories from *Group's Bible Big Books*™ create a special Bible that children want to hear and see again and again. Through the Bible stories in this book, children will learn about God's creativity, power, and great plans for us. Most importantly, kids will discover that God loves us and sent Jesus, who died for our sins.

To help children get the most from these Bible stories, each story is written in "kid-friendly," age-appropriate language that your young child can relate to and understand. Parents, Sunday school teachers, and children's workers across the country have watched delighted children learn Bible truths from *Group's Bible Big Books*—and now your child can, too! The *Pray & Play Bible for Young Children* is bursting with eye-catching, vibrant, high-quality art that entices nonreaders to explore every page in detail. But wait, there's more...

Words and pictures aren't enough to develop a passion for God's Word. Children need to use *all* of their senses to connect Bible truths to everyday life. That's why we've included three pages of activities with each story. The activities help young children and their families explore the Bible and bring it to life. Kids connect "play" with their "work" of growing up—what better way to work at learning God's Word than through play!

Since these activities have all been kid-tested, we know your child will be excited about them. Parents and teachers can be excited, too, because the activities require few supplies—most of which can be easily found around your home.

With the *Pray & Play Bible for Young Children* your child can learn Bible truths in many ways.

● Read a different story to your child each night before bed.

● Have your child "read" the pictures and tell you the stories.

● Use the *Pray & Play Bible for Young Children* as a family devotional. You can focus on one story per week and do a different activity each day, or do one activity per week (you have over a year's worth of ideas!).

● Have older children use the activities to teach a story to younger siblings.

● Sing the songs of the *Pray & Play Bible* along with the cassette—*Pray & Play Songs for Young Children*. On the cassette, you'll find thirty-seven songs from the *Pray & Play Bible* and each Bible story introduced by Chadder the Chipmunk.

The *Pray & Play Bible for Young Children* is designed to help children fall in love with God's Word. Psalm 119:105 affirms that "Your word is like a lamp for my feet and a light for my path." May God bless you as you shine his light on the little ones in your life.

● **Rhyming or musical prayers help children express praise and thanks in new ways.**
Use these songs, action rhymes, or finger play prayers to teach your child that prayer and praise are fun! Little ones will enjoy wearing out their wiggles with these active prayers, and you'll love seeing your child enthusiastic about praising God.

● **Creative prayers allow children a chance to communicate with God in meaningful ways.**
Children discover that prayer is more than a quiet time—it's an opportunity to talk to God, praise God, and thank God. Through unique prayer experiences, your child will learn that talking to God can be as simple as talking to a loving parent or friend.

● **Simple prayers teach children that they can talk to God any time, anywhere.**
Help your child understand that God is always nearby and that we can talk to God wherever we are. These child-friendly prayer ideas lend themselves to mealtimes, bedtimes...and to any other time!

● **Affirmations allow children to feel God's love in real ways.**
These unique ideas also encourage your child to express God's love to others. You'll find your child looking for positive qualities in friends, neighbors, and family members.

● **Crafts allow children to remember the Bible story through creativity.**
The crafts in this book are more than crayons, glue, and paper. They're innovative, clever, and age-appropriate activities that give kids a chance to create visual reminders of the Bible stories.

● **Service projects allow children the opportunity to act out their faith.**
What better way to help your young child develop his or her faith than by serving others. Children will understand that servanthood brings great joy!

● **Games allow kinesthetic learners the opportunity to discover more about the Bible story through action.**
We've included simple, action-packed games that will have your child smiling and learning about God's Word at the same time.

● **Singing allows musical learners to remember the Bible story through simple songs.**
These action songs will keep your child singing God's Word for days! Most children are already familiar with the simple tunes, and the words will be great reminders of each Bible story.

● **Story enhancements allow children to experience the story in new ways.**
These story enhancements use finger plays, action rhymes, and drama to help your child become a part of the story and learn to tell it again and again.

● **Snacks allow your child to create and enjoy tasty reminders of the Bible story.**
Children love to play with their food, so we've given them a wonderful excuse to do just that! What better way for children to learn Psalm 119:103, "Your promises are sweet to me, sweeter than honey in my mouth!"

God Made Our World

A long, long, time ago, before God made our world, everything was dark and empty. Then God said, "Let there be light," and light burst into the darkness.

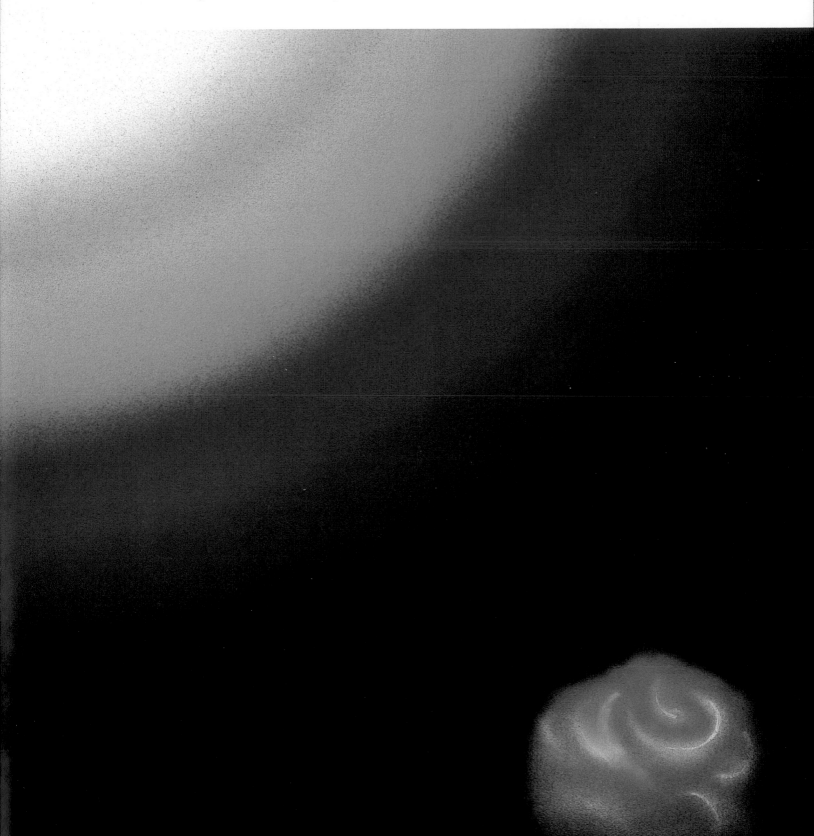

The next day, God made the bright blue sky. On the third day, God made the land and the seas and all kinds of plants and trees. Can you find all those things in this picture? Everything God made was good.

On the fourth day, God put lights in the sky. God put the bright sun in the sky for daytime. Then God made the moon and stars to twinkle in the sky during the night. God saw that the sun, moon, and stars were good.

Guess what God made on the fifth day? God made birds to fly high in the sky and fish to swim and skim through the water. How many different kinds of fish can you find in the water?

On the sixth day, God made lots more animals to live on the land. How many can you find? God saw that all the animals were good.

On the sixth day, God also created a man and a woman. Adam and Eve were the very first people in our world. Then God looked at everything he'd made and saw that it was VERY GOOD!

God made a beautiful garden for Adam and Eve to live in. God told Adam and Eve they could eat fruit from all the trees in the garden except one.

One day a snake tricked Eve into eating fruit from that special tree. Then Adam ate some, too. Because they disobeyed, God made Adam and Eve leave the garden. But God still loved them and watched over them.

God filled our world with many beautiful things. God wants us to enjoy the wonderful world he's made. God also wants us to help take care of our world. What's one thing you can do to take care of God's beautiful world?

Everything Was Good

 Lead children in the following song sung to the tune of "Old MacDonald." During the second verse, fill in the names of friends or family members.

Long ago God made the world,
And everything was good.
God made light and day and night,
And everything was good.
Growing plants,
Stars, moon, sun—
Playing in God's world is fun!
Long ago God made the world,
And everything was good.

Long ago God made the world,
And everything was good.
Animals and people, too,
And everything was good.
God made (name).
God made (name).
God made (name) and (name) and
(name).
Long ago God made the world,
And everything was good.

God Made the Animals

 Lead family members in singing the following song to the tune of "Jesus Loves Me." While you sing, have family members act out each animal mentioned in the song.

Cats and dogs and bluebirds blue,
Tigers, lions, zebras, too.
Fish and frogs and birds that fly—
So many creatures, my, oh, my!

God made the animals.
God made the animals.
God made the animals.
He made so many kinds.

Ostriches with pointy toes,
Elephants and buffaloes,
Rabbits, snakes, and kangaroos—
God made them all for me and you.

God made the animals.
God made the animals.
God made the animals.
He made so many kinds.

Psalm 19:1

 Teach your children this song sung to the tune of "The Mulberry Bush" to help them learn Psalm 19:1.

The heavens tell the glory of God,
Glory of God,
Glory of God.
The heavens tell the glory of God,
Psalm nineteen, verse one!

The skies tell what God's hands
have made,
Hands have made,
Hands have made.
The skies tell what God's hands
have made,
Psalm nineteen, verse one!

Let's Pray!

Planting Prayers

Gather seeds or bulbs, potting soil, and a large flower pot. Fill the flower pot with soil, then give each family member a few seeds or bulbs. Take turns thanking God for something in creation, such as dogs, sunshine, the ocean, or snow. As each person prays, encourage him or her to dig a hole in the soil and plant the seeds. Then pass a pitcher of water, and have them each pour a bit of water on their seeds. Family members can ask God to "grow" appealing characteristics in your family, such as kindness, patience, and love.

EXTRA IDEA! To help the seeds grow, assign a different family member to water them each day. Encourage the "seed caretaker" to pray for each family member while he or she cares for the growing plants that day.

Creation Thank You

Teach your child this simple rhyming prayer. Children enjoy filling in the names of other things that God made.

God made the sun. *(Hold arms overhead in a circle.)*
God made the sea. *(Make "waves" with arms.)*
God made the animals. *(Act like any animal—hop, growl, or rub arms to indicate "fur.")*
And God made me! *(Point to self.)*

God, thank you for the sunshine *(hold arms overhead in a circle)*
And for the deep blue sea. *(Make "waves" with arms.)*
Thanks for all the animals. *(Act like any animal.)*
And thank you, God, for me! *(Point to self.)*

EXTRA IDEA! Turn this prayer into an affirmation by substituting your child's name for the word "me."

New Ways to Pray

✔ As you read aloud "God Made Our World," pause at the end of each page. Allow children to point to items on each page, then lead them in thanking God for creating those items.

✔ Sit outside with children, and have them point out different things that God created, such as grass, flowers, clouds, animals, and people. Talk about what the world would be like if God hadn't made those things. Pray and thank God for his creativity.

✔ At mealtime or before a simple snack, help children figure out where each food item comes from. For example, they could point out that potatoes grow in the ground, oranges grow on trees, and eggs come from chickens. Lead children in thanking God for creating plants and animals that provide such tasty food.

Let's Play!

God's Fingerprints Are Everywhere

Set out an ink pad, fine-point markers, and sheets of paper. Have family members make thumb prints and fingerprints on the paper and then add ears, noses, mouths, beaks, whiskers, and tails to create a unique variety of "animal prints." Point out that God made each person's fingerprints different. Then talk about animals in creation that display God's matchless creativity, such as striped zebras, long-legged ostriches, and color-changing chameleons.

Apples Out!

 Draw an apple on a sheet of paper. Have family members work together to tape blank sheets of colorful construction paper and the apple picture in a circle on the floor. You'll need one less sheet of paper than there are players.

Play a cassette of upbeat music, and have family members hop from paper to paper. When you stop the music, the person standing on the apple must leave the game and stand outside the circle. Take away a sheet of plain paper, and continue playing until one person is left. Talk about how God sent Adam and Eve away from the garden when they sinned. Explain that even though Adam and Eve didn't live in the Garden of Eden, God still loved and cared for them.

Give God a Hand

 Use this action rhyme to help family members remember what happened on each day of creation.

One is for the day and night. (Hold up one finger.)
God knew how to make them right. (Give two thumbs up.)
Two is for the pretty sky. (Hold up two fingers.)
God made it blue—oh me, oh my! (Point to something blue.)
Three is for each flower and tree. (Hold up three fingers.)
God made them each for you and me. (Point to others.)
Four is for the moon and sun. (Hold up four fingers.)
God made them bright for everyone! (Shield eyes.)
Five is for the birds and fish (hold up five fingers),

With wings that fly and fins that swish. (Flap arms and wiggle.)
Six is for animals, people too. (Hold up six fingers.)
I'm glad that God made me and you. (Point to self, then others.)
Seven is for God's day of rest. (Hold up seven fingers.)
Thank you, God, for the world you blessed. (Fold hands.)

This is a good finger play for long car trips when you're enjoying God's creation!

A Tasty World

 Set out a variety of foods such as broccoli, carrots, pretzels, licorice, nuts, and seeds. Provide blue or green paper plates, and challenge each family member to create a colorful "world." For example, a family member might build on the plate broccoli trees, licorice snakes, and a carrot-coin sun. Children might want to create pretzel people to add to their scenes. Talk about all the yummy foods that God created when he made our world.

Sweet Reminders

 Mix equal parts of powdered sugar and peanut butter; knead the mixture to form a soft dough. Give each family member a small handful of the edible dough, and instruct them to make dough people. Set out raisins, seeds, or chocolate sprinkles to use as eyes, bellybuttons, freckles, and hair. As you work, talk about how God created us in his image. Have each person tell about his or her creation. Then enjoy the sweet treats as reminders of God's love and creativity.

One day long, long ago, God looked down on the world and saw that almost all the people were mean and bad. God felt sad and sorry that he'd ever created people. So God decided to send a flood to wash away all the bad things on earth. But one man loved God and did what was right. His name was Noah. God told Noah to build an ark so his family would be safe during the flood.

God told Noah just how to build the ark. It was a huge boat, big enough to hold Noah's family and two of every animal on earth that walks, creeps, crawls, or flies. Noah and his sons built the ark with three decks and different rooms on each deck, so Noah's family and all the animals would have a place to stay.

Tap-tap, bangety-bang, BOOM! Noah and his sons worked hard every day, and every day the ark grew larger. Noah's neighbors must have wondered why he was building such a big boat. Then, when the ark was almost finished, Noah's family began gathering food. They needed stacks and stacks and stacks of food to feed themselves and all the animals.

After months of hard work, Noah finished the ark. Then God said, "Go into the ark, you and your whole family. Seven days from now I will send rain on the earth. It will rain forty days and forty nights." So Noah and his family hurried to finish packing.

Then God did something wonderful! Way off in the distance, Noah could see the animals coming—a huge, long line of animals! God sent the animals to Noah two by two, and Noah loaded them onto the ark. When everyone was safely on board the ark, God shut the door.

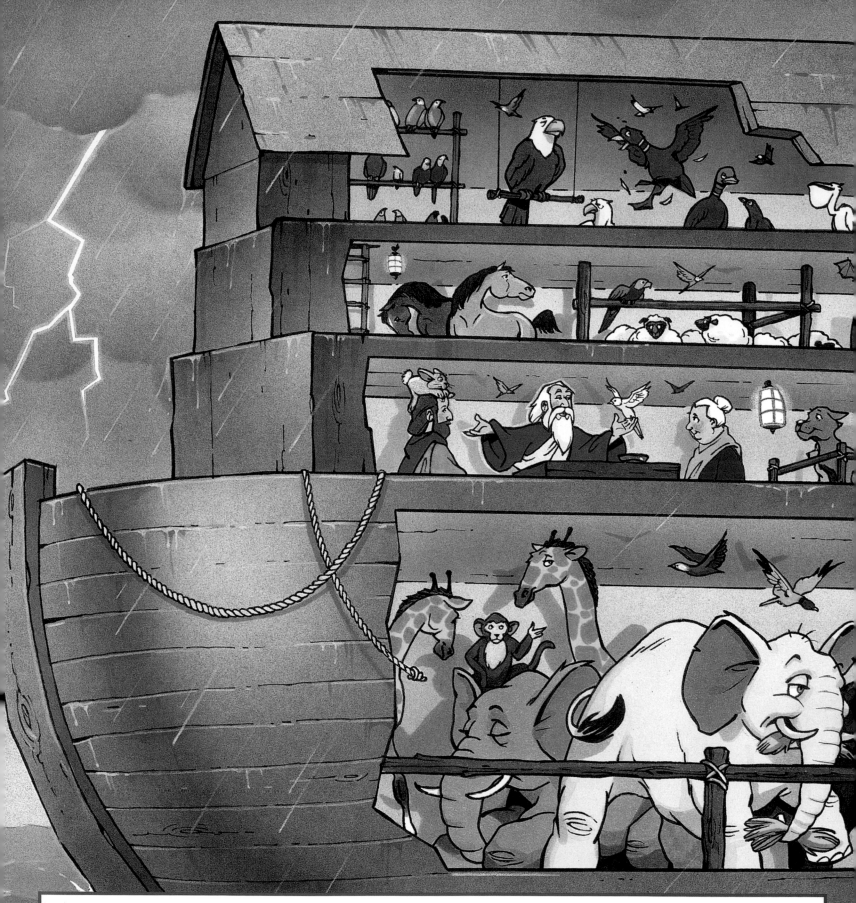

Plop-plippity-plop. The first big raindrops splashed onto the roof of the ark. Then the rain came harder and faster. The wind howled, the rain pounded, and giant crashes of thunder rocked the ark as flashes of lightning tore across the sky.

The water rose higher and higher and the ark began to float. The water kept rising until only the tips of the mountains showed. Then they, too, were swallowed by the flood. But inside the ark, everyone was safe and dry. As days turned into weeks and weeks into months, God watched over Noah and his family and all the animals on the ark.

One day the flood waters started to go down. Then—ker-THUNK! The ark bumped against a mountainside and there it came to rest. When the flood water disappeared and trees and plants began to grow again, Noah knew it was time to leave the ark. He opened the heavy door and all the animals and people came pouring out.

Noah built an altar to thank God for keeping his family safe during the flood. Then God put a shimmering rainbow in the sky as a promise never again to destroy the earth with a flood.

Did You Ever Hear?

Use these songs to remind children about all the animals that boarded Noah's ark.

Sing this song to the tune of "Did You Ever See a Lassie?"

Did you ever hear a lion,
A lion, a lion?
Did you ever hear a lion?
It sounds just like this.
(Roar like a lion.)
Did you ever hear a lion?
It sounds just like this.
(Roar like a lion.)

Did you ever hear a monkey,
A monkey, a monkey?
Did you ever hear a monkey?
It sounds just like this.
(Chatter like a monkey.)
Did you ever hear a monkey?
It sounds just like this.
(Chatter like a monkey.)

Did you ever hear an elephant,
An elephant, an elephant?
Did you ever hear an elephant?
It sounds just like this.
(Trumpet like an elephant.)
Did you ever hear an elephant?
It sounds just like this.
(Trumpet like an elephant.)

Did you ever hear a rooster,
A rooster, a rooster?
Did you ever hear a rooster?
It sounds just like this.
(Crow like a rooster.)
Did you ever hear a rooster?
It sounds just like this.
(Crow like a rooster.)

All Aboard!

This song is sung to the tune of "This Old Man."

Two by two *(link arms and take two steps)*,
Two by two *(take two more steps)*,
Look, here comes a walking zoo!
(Shield your eyes and point.)
Hear the STOMP, STOMP *(stomp your feet)*,
Flitter–flitter, flip! *(Hop and flutter your arms.)*

All aboard on Noah's ship! *(Use beckoning motion.)*

In we go *(take two steps)*,
Nice and slow *(take two more steps)*,
Careful not to step on toes! *(Jump back.)*
Hear the STOMP, STOMP *(stomp your feet)*,
Flitter–flitter, flip! *(Hop and flutter your arms.)*
All aboard on Noah's ship! *(Use beckoning motion.)*

Only God Can Make a Rainbow

This song will help children remember the importance of God's rainbow. Sing it to the tune of "Did You Ever See a Lassie?"

Only God can make a rainbow,
A rainbow, a rainbow.
Only God can make a rainbow
To shine in the sky.
Red, yellow, green, blue,
God's promise is true.
Only God can make a rainbow
To shine in the sky.

Barnyard Praise

Lead children in this action prayer to learn new ways of praising God. At the end of the rhyme, help children demonstrate ways to show their praise. You might suggest things such as clapping hands, singing, giving a hug, or shouting, "I love God!"

Horses neigh and toss their heads.
(Toss head, and act like a horse.)
Cows just sing out "moo!"
Speckled ducks quack out their thanks *("duck walk," and quack)*
Just as God made them to do.
(Point up.)

Roosters crow and strut their stuff. *(Strut like a rooster.)*
Puppies bark and play. *(Bark and jump around.)*
Animals make all that noise—
But I praise God this way...

Two by Two, I Thank You

Cut a sheet of newsprint or newspaper in half horizontally, and set one half aside. Fold the other half of the newsprint in half three or four times so you end up with a rectangle the width of the animal shapes below. Trace one of the animal shapes onto the rectangle so the dotted lines are on the folded edges. Cut out the animal, then unfold the paper to reveal four animal shapes. Make several "strings" of animals, and help children tape them together.

For each pair of animals, have each child tell you one thing to be thankful for. Write children's responses on the animals, then allow children to color the praise streamers. Hang the streamers in a prominent area. Each day allow children to tear off pairs of animals. Read the praises aloud, then encourage children to pray and thank God for the items.

New Ways to Pray

✔ Have family members take off their shoes and form a circle with their feet touching in the middle. Talk about how Noah obeyed God and followed his special instructions. Have each person wiggle his or her toes and tell one way to obey God this week. Then lead family members in prayer, asking God to help you all obey and follow him.

✔ Hug children and pray, thanking God for his love and protection.

✔ Sit under an umbrella with your children, and talk about the "storms," or prayer concerns, you and your children have. Pray and ask God to guide you through the "storms" just as he guided Noah and his family through the flood.

Animal Faces

Set out paper plates, crayons, glue sticks, yarn scraps, cotton balls, and construction paper. Demonstrate how to create an animal face by drawing eyes and a mouth on a plate, and then adding yarn or cotton balls for "fur" or torn paper for "scales." As children work, talk about all the animals that might have been on the ark—from eency weency bugs to lumbering elephants! Remind children that God took care of Noah and the animals.

EXTRA IDEA! To create masks, cut eyeholes in the paper plates before children decorate them. Family members can pair up and march into the "ark" (family car) the way the animals paraded onto Noah's ark.

It's Raining, It's Pouring!

 Set out a dishpan filled about half-way with warm water, or do this activity at bath time. Place toy boats or other floating items in the water, then give children colanders. Show children how to "fill" the colanders, then pull them out of the water so it "rains" on the boats. Explain that even though it rained on Noah's boat for forty days and nights, God took care of Noah's family and all the animals on the boat.

As children play, teach them this simple song to the tune of "Row, Row, Row Your Boat."

Sail, sail, sail the ark
O'er the ocean blue!
God's in charge of all we do
And cares for me and you!

Sail, sail, sail the ark
Up and down the sea!
God's in charge of all we do
And cares for you and me!

Safe Inside the Ark

 Using pillows and blankets, allow children to create an "ark" on a bed, under a table, or on a sofa. Then have them bring toy animals, plastic figures, and dolls aboard the ark. Be sure they fill the ark as full as possible to help them understand that there were lots and lots of animals! If possible, "board" the ark, and lead children in creating a "storm" by patting legs and clapping hands. You might even call out an occasional "BOOM!" to represent thunder.

After the storm, have everyone go outside and wave crepe paper streamers or colorful ribbons to represent the rainbow God put in the sky.

EXTRA IDEA! Go to your local library and find a cassette tape of ocean sounds. Play the cassette while your children are in the ark to give them an idea of what Noah might have heard for forty days and nights.

Rainbow of Praises

 Give each family member a sheet of red, orange, yellow, green, blue, or purple construction paper. Be sure each person has a different color. Have family members take turns telling things they love or appreciate about each other. Each time someone shares, allow family members to tear their papers. Continue until everyone has a handful of confetti. On the count of three, have everyone cheer and toss their confetti into the air, creating a rainbow of colors. Remind your family that rainbows help us remember God's love.

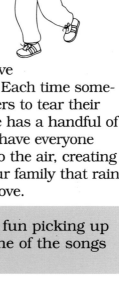

EXTRA IDEA! Have fun picking up the confetti while you sing one of the songs on page 27.

Rainbow Helping Hands

 Have each family member trace around his or her hand on a sheet of paper and then cut out the hand shape. Encourage family members to color their paper hands with rainbow colors. Demonstrate how to use a hole punch to make two holes at the wrist, then string bright yarn or ribbon through the holes to make a doorknob hanger. Have family members hang their "rainbow helping hands" in rooms they'll help out in. For example, if children hang their "helping hands" in the kitchen, they might set the table, sweep the floor, or help put groceries away.

Abraham

A long, long time ago, God asked a man named Abram to leave the beautiful city of Ur where he lived. God loved Abram, and he wanted Abram and his family to have a special place to live. God promised to show Abram the way to a new land. So Abram and his family packed up their things and got ready to move.

Abram's journey took him hundreds and hundreds of miles across a hot desert. Abram and his family and his servants and his animals walked and walked and walked and walked! One night they stopped and camped on a mountain. While they were on the mountain, Abram built an altar and worshiped God.

God blessed Abram and his nephew Lot, and they both grew wealthy. Soon they had so many animals to take care of that their shepherds couldn't find enough grass and water to feed them all.

So Abram told Lot, "Let's not fight over the land. You pick which land you want for your animals, then I'll take my animals somewhere else." Lot decided to live in the beautiful green valley. So Abram moved his family to the hills where there wasn't much food or water.

Abram trusted God to take care of him. And, sure enough, God gave Abram just what he needed. And God promised Abram that his family would grow and grow. Abram wouldn't be able to count all the people in his family, just as he couldn't count all the stars in the night sky. Then God changed Abram's name to "Abraham," which meant "father of many."

One day three special visitors came to see Abraham and Sarah. They were messengers from God. They told Abraham that Sarah would soon have a baby!

And that's just what happened! Sarah and Abraham had a little baby boy. They named him Isaac, which means "laughter," because they were so thankful and happy that God kept his promise.

God Wants Us to Follow Him

 Sing this fun action song to the tune of "Row, Row, Row Your Boat" to help children remember Abraham and Sarah's long trip. As you sing, you might march through the house pretending you're taking a trip.

> **Pack, pack, pack your bags—**
> **Now it's time to go.**
> **God wants us to follow him**
> **Because he loves us so.**
>
> **Walk, walk, walk along**
> **On the desert sand.**
> **God wants us to follow him**
> **Into a brand new land.**

God Knows Our Names

 This song will remind children that God gave Abraham a special name and that God knows each of our names, too. As you sing this song to the tune of "London Bridge," fill in the names of friends and family members.

> **God loves** (name) **and** (name) **and**
> **(name).**
> **God loves** (name).
> **God loves** (name).
> **God loves** (name) **and** (name) **and**
> **(name).**
> **He knows our names.**

> **God loves** (name) **and** (name) **and**
> **(name).**
> **God loves** (name).
> **God loves** (name).
> **God loves** (name) **and** (name) **and**
> **(name).**
> **He knows our names.**

Trust the Lord

 Use this song to teach children to trust and obey God just as Abraham did. Sing it to the tune of "Frère Jacques."

> **Trust the Lord, trust the Lord,**
> **Every day, every way.**
> **Turn to him and pray.**
> **Trust him and obey,**
> **Every day, every way.**

Let's Pray!

A Sky Full of Promises

Gather around a large sheet of blue or black paper. As family members take turns naming prayer concerns, use white chalk to write the concerns on the paper. (Be sure to scatter the requests randomly on the sheet, rather than making a list.) Have family members join hands around the sheet of paper and take turns praying for each concern. Then post the paper in a prominent place. In the coming weeks, watch how God answers each request or concern. When family members see an answer to prayer, have someone place a foil star sticker over that request. Your family will soon see that God keeps his promises and listens when we pray.

I Love You!

Teach children this prayer sung to the tune of "Jesus Loves Me." Before you sing, remind them of prayers that God has answered. Then allow them to pray about any concerns they might have.

Thank you, God, for answered
   prayers.
Thanks for being everywhere.
Thanks for listening when I pray.
I know you hear each word I say.

Chorus:
Oh, God, I love you.
Oh, God, I love you.
Oh, God, I love you.
You hear me when I pray.

New Ways to Pray

✔ Talk about the great big family that God promised Abraham. Then join hands and thank God for each member of your family.

✔ Before each car trip, allow a family member to pray for safety on your "journey"—even if it's just to the corner grocery store! Remind your children that God protected Abraham on a long trip.

✔ As a family, look through photo albums and pause to pray for each family member. Children may want to call relatives who live far away to learn specific prayer requests.

Let's Play!

You're a Star!

God promised to increase Abraham's family so that it would be like the stars in the sky—too numerous to count. You can help children understand that they are special in God's family. Set out aluminum foil, kite string, and a cro- chet hook or knitting needle. Allow each child to crumple and flatten the foil to sculpt ten to twenty star shapes. Use the crochet hook to poke a hole at the top of each star, then carefully thread a twelve- to fourteen-inch length of kite string through each hole. Help children hang the stars from their bedroom ceilings. The "starry skies" will help teach children that God keeps his promises to us just as he did to Abraham.

Starry Sky

Help children use sharpened pencils to carefully punch about twenty holes in the bottom of a shoe box. As you work together, talk about the special members in your family. See if you can name a different family member for each hole you punch in the box! Go to a room that can be completely darkened, such as a closet or basement, and turn off the lights. Show children how to shine a flashlight into the box so the light shines through the holes—just like a starry sky. Explain that God told Abraham that he'd have many family members—even more than the stars in the sky!

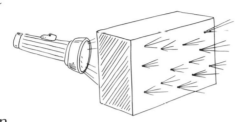

EXTRA IDEA! Older children might enjoy a more challenging twist on this activity. Fill clean, empty soup cans with water, then freeze them. Help children hammer nails into the cans to make "stars." Allow the ice to melt and the cans to dry completely, then have children paint the outside of the cans black or blue. (Watch out for sharp edges inside the cans.) Instruct children to place votive candles inside the cans. When the candles are lit, they will look like stars glowing on a clear night!

Follow the Footprints

Have each family member trace his or her feet on brown grocery sacks and then cut out the footprints. You might want to have everyone make two or three pairs of feet.

Give all the footprints to one person, and have everyone else hide in one room. Instruct the "path maker" to use the footprints to make a path through the house or outside. After a minute, family members may follow the footprints to find the path maker. As you take turns following the footprints, talk about how Abraham followed God's instructions even when he didn't know where God would lead him.

Praise Altar

Take a walk, and look for fist-sized stones. You'll need quite a few, so it might be a good idea to collect them in a wagon. When you return home, gather family members outside and form a circle. Explain that Abraham made an altar to praise and worship God. To help children understand what an altar was, give each family member a handful of stones. Go around the circle and have each person praise God for one blessing, such as a great family, a warm home, a good teacher, or for Jesus. As each person names a praise, have him or her place a stone on the ground so the stones form a pile. Close by singing a praise song such as "God Is So Good" or "Great Is Thy Faithfulness."

EXTRA IDEA! Leave your "Praise Altar" standing, with a pile of stones nearby. Each time a family member thinks of something else to praise God for, he or she can add another stone to the altar.

Graham Cracker Tents

Give each person three graham cracker squares and a paper plate. Set out marshmallow creme and plastic knives. Demonstrate how to make a "tent." Lay one graham cracker flat on the plate. Then spread marshmallow creme on the other two crackers, and lean them together, as shown. As family members enjoy their tent treats, explain that Abraham and Sarah moved and traveled and lived in tents much of the time.

Welcome, Neighbors!

Abraham and Sarah were strangers in a new land. You can welcome newcomers to your neighborhood by creating a welcome basket. Have your family work together to fill a basket or grocery sack with goodies, welcome signs, and gift certificates to local restaurants or grocery stores. Younger children can help by decorating the basket with ribbon or by coloring the grocery sack.

· Moses ·

One day as Moses was watching his sheep, he saw a strange sight. Bright flames of fire burned from a nearby bush, but the bush didn't burn up! When Moses took a closer look, he heard the voice of God! God wanted Moses to go to Egypt and tell King Pharaoh to let God's people go. Pharaoh was mean—he made God's people work as slaves. God promised to help Moses, so Moses set off to see Pharaoh.

MOSES warned Pharaoh that if he didn't let God's people go, bad things would happen. But Pharaoh wouldn't listen. So God sent swarming bugs; thousands of hopping, croaking frogs; and pounding hailstorms. Finally, after lots and lots of bad things happened, Pharaoh agreed to let God's people go.

So Moses led God's people out of Egypt. But then, mean old Pharaoh changed his mind. He sent his army to bring the people back. Then God sent a big wind to split the sea in two so the people could walk across on dry ground and get away from Pharaoh's soldiers. When Pharaoh's soldiers stepped onto the path, the water came crashing down!

After God's people escaped from Egypt, they camped in the desert. Then Moses went up on a mountain to talk to God. God gave Moses special rules for everyone to follow. We call those rules the Ten Commandments.

When Moses came down from the mountain with the Ten Commandments, he saw the people worshiping a golden calf! This made God very sad. God wants us to love and worship him. He wants to be the most important part of our lives.

God wants us to follow the Ten Commandments, too. Following the Ten Commandments shows that we love God. Can you find the children in this picture who are showing their love for God? What other ways can you show your love for God?

The Ten Commandments can also help us remember to love others. God wants us to love our families, our friends, and even people we don't know! Can you find the children in this picture who are showing love for others? How can you show your love for others?

The Ten Commandments help us remember to love God and love others. Let's read the commandments together.

God Told Moses

This song will help children understand that God called Moses to do an important job. Sing it to the tune of "Did You Ever See a Lassie?"

God told Moses, "Take my people
From Pharaoh–he's evil!"
God told Moses, "Take my people
From Pharaoh right now!"

So Moses told Pharaoh,
"The Israelites must go."
But old Pharaoh, he said,
"Oh no! They're staying with me!"

God sent frogs and gnats and
locusts
And flies and diseases.
Finally Pharaoh changed his mind
When his firstborn son died.

So Pharaoh told Moses,
"Take God's people–please go!"
So the Israelites were free
To go worship the Lord.

I Can Trust God

Use this song to teach children the importance of trusting God and his rules. Sing it to the tune of "Jesus Loves Me."

I can trust God–so can you–
When he gives us a job to do.
In hard times or when you're scared,
Trust that God will be right there.

Yes, I can trust God.
Yes, you can trust God.
We all can trust God.
He'll always be right here.

God's commands are always good.
They help us live the way we should.
God will give us what we need.
When we trust God, we'll succeed.

Yes, I can trust God.
Yes, you can trust God.
We all can trust God.
He'll always be right here.

The Ten Commandments Song

Use this song, sung to the tune of "Ten Little Indians," to teach your children more about the Ten Commandments—God's special rules.

I'm your only God–it's true. *(Hold up one finger.)*
Never worship idols–ooh! *(Hold up two fingers.)*
Respect my name, and don't be rude. *(Hold up three fingers.)*
Keep the Sabbath holy. *(Hold up four fingers.)*

Please obey your mom and dad. *(Hold up five fingers.)*
Don't kill people–oh! how bad! *(Hold up six fingers, and shake your head.)*
Please stay married–you'll be glad. *(Hold up seven fingers.)*
Don't steal things from others. *(Hold up eight fingers.)*

Never, ever tell a lie. *(Hold up nine fingers.)*
Don't wish for things your neighbors buy. *(Hold up ten fingers.)*
When you follow God's rules, you'll be *(clap your hands)*
Safe and very hap-py! *(Turn in a circle, then clap one time.)*

Let's Pray!

Praise Balloons

Blow up and tie off one balloon for each person. Give each family member a permanent marker, and have him or her draw a smiley face on the balloon. You may want to provide crepe paper streamers or yarn for indi-

viduals to tape on as "hair." When everyone has designed a balloon, form a circle. Go around the circle, and have each family member say one great thing about God, such as "God is powerful," "God is creative," or "God is loving." As family members praise God, have them bop their balloons into the circle. Soon you'll be bopping balloons and celebrating our one, true God! Close by having everyone sit on a balloon to pop it and then say, "Amen!" (Have family members pick up all the balloon bits so toddlers or animals don't choke on them.)

Counting Commandments

Use this simple counting rhyme to teach children that God's ten special rules help us follow him. Children can hold up the appropriate number of fingers for each line.

One, two,
One, two, three.
Your special rules are just for me!
   (Point to self.)
Three, four,
Three, four, five.
As I grow, they'll be my guide.
   (Move hands up to indicate growth.)
Five, six,
Five, six, seven.
Your special rules came straight
   from heaven! *(Point up.)*
Seven, eight,
Seven, eight, nine.
I'll keep them in my heart and
   mind. *(Touch chest, then head.)*
Nine, ten.
That's the end! *(Clap on each word.)*
I'll thank you for your rules again!
   (Wiggle ten fingers.)

New Ways to Pray

✔ Lead children in praying for the law enforcement officials in your community. Thank God for allowing us to live in a country where laws and rules keep us safe and give us the freedom to worship God.

✔ Light a candle, and talk about how God spoke to Moses from a burning bush. Have family members pray and ask God to open their ears to listen for his voice each day.

✔ Have each child ask God to help him or her show love to one specific person this week. Then pray and commit to showing love for God in a new way each day.

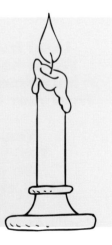

Let's Play!

Path Through the Sea

Have each child use a white crayon to color a one-inch line down the middle of a sheet of white paper. Encourage them to press down firmly on the crayons. Set out blue watercolor paint and a paintbrush. Show children how to paint the paper and watch the "path" appear in the middle of the "sea" where the crayon resists the paint. Remind them that God provided a dry path for the Israelites to walk on as they escaped Pharaoh's army.

EXTRA IDEA! Use this same idea to teach children how manna miraculously appeared each day. Have children use white crayons to draw food on white paper. Explain that God sent special food for his people every day. Then have children paint over the paper with brown watercolor paint. Children will see "manna" appear in the "desert" just as the Israelites did!

Musical Sabbath Chairs

Form a circle of chairs that face outward, using one fewer chair than the number of family members. Play a cassette of upbeat music, and have family members skip, hop, or tiptoe around the circle. Explain that when you pause the cassette and call out "Sabbath," each family member must sit in a chair as quickly as possible to remember that God wants us to rest on the Sabbath. When family members have taken all the available seats, have the person who didn't find a seat name one of God's special rules. Continue playing until you've named all of God's rules.

Red Sea Rhyme

Lead children in the following finger play. Be sure to repeat the rhyme several times to help them learn it.

Moses and God's people (hold up your thumb and wiggle your fingers)
Stood beside the sea. (Hold your hand in front of you.)
"How can we get across?" (turn your palm upward)
They asked unhappily. (Make a fist, and wipe your eyes.)
Then God told Moses (hold up your thumb)
To lift the staff in his hand. (Hold up your hand.)
Then the water split apart (bring palms together, then part them)
And made a path of dry land. ("Walk" your fingers down your arm.)
The people were so happy (wiggle your fingers)
That they began to sing (wiggle your fingers),
"Thank you, God, for your great love. (Cover your heart.)
You CAN do anything!" (Clap your hands.)

Burning Bushes

Shake flaked coconut in a plastic bag with a few drops of red food coloring. Have children help you clean stalks of celery, keeping the leaves on the celery tops.

Set out softened cream cheese, plastic knives, and a bowl of the red coconut "flames." Let children fill the celery stalk centers with cream cheese. Then demonstrate how to dab a little cream cheese on the celery leaves, too. Have children sprinkle red coconut flames on their celery "bushes." Remind them that God spoke to Moses through a burning bush and asked Moses to be his special helper.

Coloring Tablets

Help each child mix six tablespoons vegetable oil, one-half cup cornstarch, and a few drops red food coloring in a sealable plastic bag. Have them knead the mixture until it's smooth and then let the excess air out of the bags. Seal the bags, then tape them securely with clear packing tape. Explain that God "wrote" his special rules on stone tablets because he loves us so much. On their "coloring tablets," have your children take turns drawing hearts, happy faces, flowers, and other designs by running a finger across the plastic bag. With each new design, say, "You're special because..."

Every year Hannah and her husband traveled to the house of the Lord to worship. But Hannah never had a baby to take with her. This made Hannah very sad. Sometimes she got so sad she couldn't even eat.

Hannah prayed and told God how sad she was.
She asked God to give her a son. She promised
God that if he gave her a son, she
would bring him to live in the
house of the Lord where he
could serve God all his life.

God heard Hannah and answered her prayer! Soon Hannah and her husband, Elkanah, had a baby boy. Hannah named the baby Samuel, which means "God heard."

Hannah kept her promise to give Samuel back to God. As soon as Samuel was big enough, Hannah took him to live in the house of the Lord. Hannah knew that Eli, the kind old priest, would take good care of Samuel.

Every year when she came to worship God, Hannah brought Samuel a new coat. Hannah was happy to see Samuel. She was glad to know Samuel was learning about God as he served as a helper in the house of the Lord.

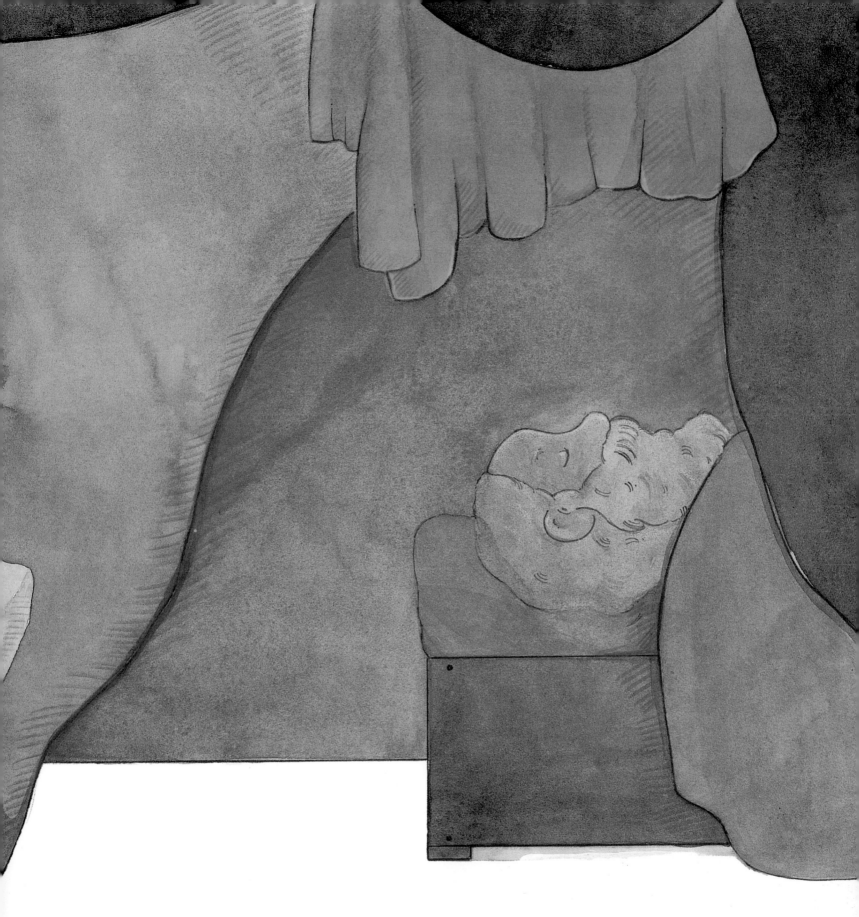

One night God spoke to Samuel. At first Samuel thought it was Eli's voice he was hearing. But Eli knew the voice was God calling. He told Samuel to answer, "Speak, Lord. I'm listening."

God gave Samuel a message to give to Eli. Samuel obeyed God and gave Eli the message. As Samuel grew up, God talked to him many more times, and Samuel became a great leader for God's people. We can trust God and listen to God, just as Samuel did.

We Can Listen

Use this song to help children remember that God wants us to listen to him and pray. Sing this song to the tune of "Old MacDonald."

We can listen to God's Word
And talk to God each day.
When we hear stories from God's Word,
We'll listen and obey.
If we open up our ears,
God's Word is loud and clear.
We can listen to God's Word
And talk to God each day.

We can listen to God's Word
And talk to God each day.
When we hear stories from God's Word,
We'll listen and obey.
If we open up our ears,
God's Word is loud and clear.
We can listen to God's Word
And talk to God each day.

Growing in God's Love

This song is a great affirmation to small children! Sing it to the tune of "Jesus Loves Me."

God can help me as I grow
And teach me things that I should know.
As I listen, as I pray,
I'm growing inside every day.

Growing in God's love,
Growing in God's love,
Growing in God's love—
God helps me grow each day.

Growing taller every day.
Growing outside many ways.
God sees everything I do.
He knows I'm growing inside, too.

Growing in God's love,
Growing in God's love,
Growing in God's love—
God helps me grow each day.

Let's Pray!

Prayer Quilt

Use this craft prayer to remind children that they are covered with God's love day and night. Set out paper, scissors, a glue stick, markers or crayons, a gingerbread man cookie cutter, and a variety of fabric scraps. Show children how to trace around the cookie cutter and cut out the shape. Allow a

few moments for children to create paper versions of themselves. Then have them glue two-by-two-inch squares of fabric on sheets of paper to create "quilts" for their paper dolls. As each child glues a square, have him or her complete the sentence, "I'm thankful that God..." When the quilt is finished, each child will have a visual picture of being covered with God's love!

Help Me Listen

Teach children this simple prayer. Talk about the importance of listening to God and being used by God.

God, help me listen when you call.
For even though I'm very small,
You can use my hands and feet
To show your love to those I meet.

New Ways to Pray

✔ Before bedtime lie on each child's bed and pray with him or her. Point out that Samuel was asleep when God gave him an important message.

✔ Each night tell children one way you've "heard" or "seen" God that day. Pray and ask God to use you and your children to help others see and hear God, too.

✔ Look through photographs of your children and talk with them about the things they can do now that their bigger. Have them thank God for helping them as they grow.

Let's Play!

Apple Ears

Give each child a napkin, a round cracker, two raisins, and two apple wedges. Show children how to make cracker faces with raisin eyes and apple ears. As children enjoy their snacks, talk about how Samuel listened when God spoke to him.

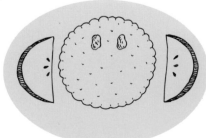

Listen to the Lord

Use this action rhyme to help children remember the importance of listening and praying to God.

I listen up high. (Stand on tiptoe, and cup hands around ears.)
I listen down low. (Crouch down, and cup hands around ears.)
I listen to the Lord (stand up, and cup hands around ears)
Everywhere I go. (Turn in a circle.)

I talk up high. (Speak in a high-pitched voice.)
I talk down low. (Speak in a deep voice.)
I talk to the Lord (fold hands in prayer)
Everywhere I go. (Turn in a circle.)

Colorful Coats

 Set out fabric paints, glitter glue, fake jewels, and an old, oversized t-shirt for each family member. Draw names out of a hat to determine who will make a colorful "coat" for another family member. As you're designing the coats, talk about how Hannah brought Samuel a new coat while he was living with Eli.

Mystery Messages

 Put a blank cassette tape into a cassette player. Have family members take turns calling each other's names into the microphone. Encourage family members to disguise their voices. Then listen to the cassette together, and try to figure out who's voice is calling. Remind children that God called Samuel because he had an important message for Samuel.

Nursery Helpers

 When Hannah had a baby boy, she kept her promise to God and sent Samuel to live in God's house. You can help the babies and children who are growing up in your church, too. Plan a day to clean the nursery and toddler rooms at church. Even the smallest children can scrub tables and put toys away while adults vacuum, sweep, or mop. Donate a supply of cookies and juice, anti-bacterial soap, or even a few toys. Whenever you visit the nursery, remember Hannah's promise to God.

EXTRA IDEA! Most churches can use helpers every day, doing everything from painting to vacuuming to sorting through Sunday school materials. See what other ways you can be helpers in God's house.

Growing in God's Love

 Cut a large heart from red construction paper, then write "Growing in God's Love" on the heart. Tape four sheets of white paper together, end to end, then tape the heart to the top. Post the finished paper strip to a wall so the bottom sheet of paper is touching the floor. Explain that just as Samuel grew up in God's house, we can grow in God's love. Every month have children stand against the paper strip. Make hearts to indicate children's heights. Next to each heart, write something you love and appreciate about that child.

EXTRA IDEA! Adults can grow in God's love too. Each time you write affirmations next to children's heights, have each child write or draw (or dictate while you write) one way he or she has seen you show God's love. Children might notice things such as a warm hug, a smile, or a forgiving heart.

Esther

King Xerxes of Persia needed a queen—
Someone who was kind and lovely to be seen.
So young women came from nations all around;
Surely from among them a queen could be found.
Young Esther was brought by her cousin Mordecai,
And she was the one who caught the king's eye.
On Esther's lovely head, the king placed a crown.
Then all the happy people cheered and bowed down.

Now a man named Haman was haughty and proud.
Most people bowed when he walked through a crowd.
But Mordecai wouldn't bow—no sirree!
He would only bow down to God, you see.
Evil Haman fumed when he saw Mordecai.
Haman said, "I'll make a plan to get rid of that guy!"

So nasty Haman cooked up a horrible, wicked plan
To kill all the Jews who lived in the land.
When Mordecai heard what would happen to the Jews,
He quickly sent a message to give Esther the news.
"Please talk to the king," his urgent message said.
"If you don't, all Jewish people will end up dead!"

Esther was frightened—what should she do?
Haman didn't know that she was a Jew.
But going to the king was a dangerous task;
No one could see him unless they'd been asked.
The penalty was death if the king said, "Go away."
So Esther asked for all the Jewish people to pray.

Then into the throne room walked the brave queen.
The king thought, "It's Esther—what could this mean?"
King Xerxes smiled to her and held out his scepter
To show that he was very glad to see her and accept her.
"Please come to a banquet I'm preparing for you,"
Said Esther. Then she added, "Please bring Haman, too."

So Haman and the king went and visited the queen.
"How nice to be with you!" Haman boasted and preened.
Then Queen Esther asked them to return the next day, too.
Said the king, "Dear Esther, what can I do for you?"
"All my people will be killed," Esther told the king.
Then he asked, "Who would do such a terrible thing?"

"This man—Haman!" Esther said accusingly.
"This horrible person is my people's enemy."
Then the king called his servants and said what must be done.
"Take this man, and hang him before the day is done!"

Then throughout the kingdom this happy
message spread:
"Queen Esther has saved us! Our enemy
is dead!"
The Jewish people praised the Lord in happy
celebration.
"Praise our Lord, and praise the queen who
bravely saved our nation!"
And even now, the Jewish people celebrate
this way—
The joyous feast of Purim is a happy holiday!

Queen Esther

Teach children this song to reinforce the story of brave Queen Esther. Remind your child that Esther's name means "star." Sing the song to the tune of "Did You Ever See a Lassie?"

Did you hear about Queen Esther
(cup hand to right ear),
Queen Esther, Queen Esther?
Did you hear about Queen Esther?
(Cup hand to left ear.)
(Clap, clap) **She's a star!** *(Flick fingers on each word.)*

Queen Esther was so brave.
(Flex muscles.)
She knew that she must save
(put index finger to temple)
All her people from old Haman
(point to others),
So they would not die! *(Put hand on head.)*

Did you hear about Queen Esther
(cup hand to right ear),
Queen Esther, Queen Esther?
Did you hear about Queen Esther?
(Cup hand to left ear.)
(Clap, clap) **She's a star!** *(Flick fingers on each word.)*

The great celebration *(raise hands and wiggle fingers)*
All over the nation *(turn in a circle)*
Was to help the Jews remember
(put index finger to temple)
Queen Esther, the star! *(Flick fingers on each word.)*

God's Plans

This song will remind children that God has plans for us just as he had special plans for Esther. Sing this song to the tune of "This Old Man."

God has plans
That we'll see—
Special plans for you and me.
Jump up, clap three times *(jump up, then clap three times),*
Now slap on your knees! *(Pat hands on knees.)*
Celebrate God's plans with me.

Special plans
For work and play
And helping friends along the way.
Jump up, clap three times *(jump up, then clap three times),*
Now let's shout, "Hooray!" *(Raise arms and shout, "Hooray!")*
Celebrate God's plans today!

I Am Special

Use this song to help your children realize that they are special. Sing it to the tune of "Frère Jacques."

I am special, I am special.
If you look, you will see
Someone very special,
Someone very special.
God made me. God made me.

Let's Pray!

Thankful Crowns

Set out glitter glue, fake jewels, and two-by-twenty-inch strips of construction paper. Explain that you're going to make crowns that look like what Queen Esther might have worn. Talk about how family members and friends are like "jewels" that God gives us. Have each family member pray and thank God for each "jewel" in his or her life. Then instruct individuals to add a jewel to the paper "crown" for each person they've prayed for. Have them staple the ends of the paper together to create wearable reminders of your "royal" family!

Worship Prayer

Use this action prayer to help children worship God. Be sure to repeat the rhyme several times so they learn the words and actions.

Oh, God, you made the starry sky.
(Flick fingers in air like twinkling stars.)
You made the mighty sea. *(Wave arms like ocean waves.)*
You took care of your people *(spread arms wide),*
And you take care of me. *(Hug yourself.)*

Thank you, God, for the starry sky *(flick fingers in air like twinkling stars)*
And for the mighty sea. *(Wave arms like ocean waves.)*
Thanks for loving your people *(hold arms in a heart shape),*
And thanks for loving me. *(Hug self.)*

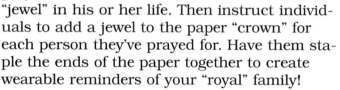

New Ways to Pray

✔ When Esther approached the king's throne to ask him something important, he extended his scepter as a way of welcoming her. Have your family pass around a broom "scepter" and pray for specific needs. Family members might ask God to heal a sick friend, help a hurting relative, or guide them through a difficult situation. Thank God for welcoming us when we come before him.

✔ Allow each family member a special night to be a king or a queen. Have the king or queen sit in a "throne" while family members pray and thank God for him or her.

✔ As a family, link arms and pray that God would help you work together just as Esther and Mordecai worked together.

Let's Play!

Kingly Rings

Set out modeling dough, three-inch pieces of chenille wire, and a bowl of large pasta wheels. Demonstrate how to make a ring by setting a pasta wheel on the lower part of one finger. Then put both ends of the chenille wire through the wheel, and twist the wire together underneath the finger. Allow children to make "seals" by pressing their rings into the modeling dough. Explain that the king gave Mordecai his ring so Mordecai could make a new law for the Jews.

Teamwork!

 Have family members form pairs. (If you have an uneven number of people, form a trio.) Have partners stand facing each other, hands joined, then slip rubber bands over their wrists. Give each pair a different task to do such as wrapping a birthday gift, fixing a snack for everyone, raking leaves, or making a bed. Have family members watch each pair find ways to work together and accomplish their task. Talk about how Mordecai and Esther worked together to save the Jews.

EXTRA IDEA! For a fun (and silly) family night, try to eat dinner with your wrists linked together. Not only will everyone get a lot of laughs, but you'll also get a hands-on lesson in teamwork!

Good King, May I?

 Provide fake jewels, a bathrobe, and a paper crown. Have one family member dress up like a king or queen. Send the "Good King" or "Good Queen" to one end of a room, and have him or her sit on a "throne." Have everyone else line up at the opposite end of the room. Allow family members to take turns asking, "Good King (or "Good Queen"), may I come closer?" The Good King (or Good Queen) must answer, "Yes, good servant, you may." Then have the king or queen tell how many and what kind of steps the player may take, such as three baby steps, two large steps, or one hop.

The first person to reach the throne becomes the new king or queen. Explain that Esther had to ask the king for something important.

Bagel Crowns

 Give each child half of a bagel. Let him or her spread jelly over the top of the bagel and arrange golden raisin "jewels" around the edge to make a crown. Talk about what it would have been like for Esther to suddenly become a queen!

EXTRA IDEA! Turn your snack time into an affirmation time. Each time you add a jewel to your bagel crown, tell each child one reason that he or she is a jewel in your life.

You're a Star!

 Roll out refrigerator cookie dough, and have family members take turns using a star-shaped cookie cutter to make star cookies. As you're working, talk about the fact that Esther's name means "star." Bake the cookies, then allow them to cool completely. Set out a variety of decorating items such as frosting, colored sprinkles, cinnamon-heart candies, and 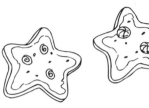 M&M's. Have each family member decorate a star cookie for another family member so each person has a special cookie. Talk about how each of us is a "star" and that God can use us just as he used Queen Esther.

EXTRA IDEA! Get a book of names from your local library, and tell each family member what his or her name means. You might tell children why you chose their names or an interesting story about your own name.

Star Messengers

 Mordecai and Esther worked together by sending messages back and forth. Your family can send messages to help and encourage others. Have family members cut star shapes from shiny wrapping paper. (The shapes should be about the size of an adult's hand.) Then use markers or glitter glue to write notes of encouragement to a pastor, teacher, friend, relative, or neighbor. Place each note inside an envelope, then have children decorate the envelopes with foil star stickers. Your messages will make others feel like shining stars!

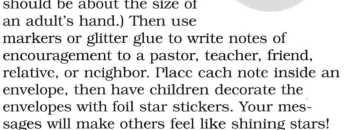

God wanted Jonah to go preach to the people of Nineveh. But Jonah didn't want to go. He decided to run away instead. Jonah thought that if he ran far enough, he could run away from God. So he got on a boat that was going all the way across the sea.

Jonah didn't want God to find him, so he went down far inside the boat. He lay down there and fell fast asleep.

A big storm blew up, and the sailors were afraid the boat would sink. They asked Jonah to pray for the storm to go away. But Jonah knew God had sent the storm. He told the sailors, "Throw me overboard. Then the storm will stop." The sailors didn't want to throw Jonah overboard, but they were afraid of the storm. So they picked up Jonah and threw him into the stormy sea. Kersplash!

Jonah began to sink into the cold, dark water. Deeper and deeper he went. But he didn't drown. God sent a big fish to swallow him up. Gulp, gulp, gulp! Jonah stayed inside the fish for three days and three nights.

While Jonah was inside the fish, he prayed. He thanked God for saving him from drowning in the sea. He told God, "I'll do what you want me to do."

God heard Jonah's prayer. And guess what happened next? The fish spit Jonah out. Kerthunk! Jonah ended up on dry land. He was glad to be out of that fish!

Jonah obeyed God and went straight to Nineveh. He told the people there to believe in God. The people listened to everything Jonah said. They stopped doing bad things and believed in God.

Forgiveness Song

Sing this song to the tune of "Jesus Loves Me" as a reminder to your children that God forgives us.

Silly Jonah ran away (*run in place*),
But God still watched him day by day. (*Shield eyes with hand, as if searching.*)
Jonah prayed inside a whale (*fold hands in prayer*),
And God's forgiveness never failed. (*Shake head "no."*)

God will forgive us. (*Cross arms over heart.*)
God will forgive us.
God will forgive us
When we ask him to. (*Fold hands in prayer.*)

Like Jonah we may disobey (*shake index finger*),
But God forgives us when we pray. (*Fold hands in prayer.*)
Even if we try to hide (*cover face with hands*),
God will still be on our side. (*Hug self.*)

God will forgive us. (*Cross arms over chest.*)
God will forgive us.
God will forgive us
When we ask him to. (*Fold hands in prayer.*)

Runaway Jonah

This song will allow your children to act out the story of Jonah. Sing it to the tune of "London Bridge."

Jonah runs and hides from God. (*Cover face with hands.*)
Where is he? (*Shield eyes with hand.*)
Can you see? (*Shield eyes with hand.*)
Jonah runs and hides from God (*cover face with hands*),
But God forgives him. (*Cross hands over heart.*)

In the belly of a fish (*hold nose*),
Jonah prays (*fold hands in prayer*)
Three whole days. (*Hold up three fingers.*)
In the belly of a fish (*hold nose*),
And God forgives him. (*Cross hands over heart.*)

I'll Pray

Sing this song with children about the importance of prayer. Sing it to the tune of "Jesus Loves Me."

God wants me to always pray;
No matter what the people say.
God will answer all my cares,
When I offer him my prayers.
Yes, God, I'll pray.
Yes, God, I'll pray.
Yes, God, I'll pray.
I'll pray to only you.

Let's Pray!

God Is With Us

Teach children this song to encourage them to pray for friends and family members each day. Sing it to the tune of "Jesus Loves Me."

Whether I'm at home or play,
God is with me every day.
Thank you, God, for being near.
When I pray, I know you hear.

Chorus:
I pray for (name).
I pray for (name).
I pray for (name).
God, watch over them today.

Anywhere Prayers

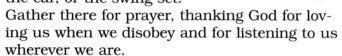

As a reminder that Jonah talked to God from inside a great fish, find interesting and unique places for family prayer time. Allow each family member to find a spot such as a closet, a treehouse, the car, or the swing set. Gather there for prayer, thanking God for loving us when we disobey and for listening to us wherever we are.

EXTRA IDEA!

Just as God sent Jonah far away, extend your "anywhere prayers" far outside the home. Think of places in your community and outside your community where you can pray, such as schools, libraries, restaurants, doctors' offices, courthouses, or police stations. Take your family to a new place each day and pray for the people at that place.

New Ways to Pray

✔ Help children pray for people of different faiths. Pray that all people would come to understand that there's only one true God.

✔ Just as God called Jonah to reach a wicked city, God calls us to be lights in a dark world. With your children, look over a newspaper and point out stories of people living with the consequences of sin. (Be sure to choose stories that aren't disturbing or frightening to young children.) Pray for the people mentioned in the stories.

✔ On your refrigerator, post pictures of missionaries that you or your church supports. Talk about where they live and the struggles they might be facing. Have children pray for the missionaries and for the people that they're ministering to.

Let's Play!

Rock the Boat

Sit on the floor, facing your child with your legs apart and feet touching. Hold hands and gently rock back and forth as you sing "Row, Row, Row Your Boat." Remind your child of the storm that rocked Jonah's boat. Then change the words and sing, "Tip, tip, tip your boat..." and then, "Rock, rock, rock your boat..."

Big Fish Puppet

 Give each child a business-size envelope, and have him or her seal it shut. Help each child cut one end off the envelope, about one-half inch from the edge. Then demonstrate how to cut out a triangle mouth from the other end. Set out markers, glitter glue, crayons, and other art supplies, and have children decorate their fish.

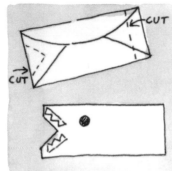 Have each child put one hand and arm in the envelope to make the fish come "alive." Then show them how your fish puppet can "swallow" the fingers of your other hand!

EXTRA IDEA! Use the puppet fish to get household chores "gobbled up" and done with a smile. On slips of paper, write down (or draw a picture of) household tasks, such as clearing the table, making beds, sweeping the floor, or watering flowers. Place the slips on the floor, and have children wear their puppet fish to "swallow" tasks they would like to do. Talk about how Jonah was swallowed by a fish when he didn't do the task God set before him.

Runaway Game

 Use this game to help children remember that even though Jonah ran away, God forgave him. Have family members form a circle and put their hands behind their backs. Choose someone to be "Jonah," and give Jonah an object such as a plastic ball or small toy. Jonah will carry the object around the outside of the circle, while family members say, "Jonah, Jonah disobeyed. God forgave him anyway." At the end of the phrase, Jonah will put the object into another family member's hands, and that person will chase Jonah around the circle. If Jonah makes it back to the open spot in the circle without being tagged, the person holding the object will be Jonah.

Fish Food

 Set out tuna salad, bread, and a heart-shaped cookie cutter. Have children cut the bread with the cookie cutter, then spread tuna salad on each piece of bread. Point out that when you turn the heart-shape on its side, it looks like a fish. (The pointed end is the face, the rounded end represents the fins.) Have children place a gummy bear on each fish snack to represent Jonah in the belly of the great fish.

Hug-and-Seek

 Play this variation of Hide-and-Seek to help children learn that we can't hide from God and that God loves us. Have family members hide while you count to ten. Each time you find a family member, give him or her a hug and say, "God sees you and so do I." Then have that person help you find the others. As you find each person, give group hugs and say together, "God sees you and so do we."

Fish Bank

 Set out construction paper; markers; glue sticks; and a clean, empty two-liter bottle. Lay the bottle on its side, then have family members work together to decorate it so it looks like a fish. As you work, talk about how hard it might be to go to a faraway place to tell people about God's love. Place the completed "fish bank" on the table. Encourage children to look for spare change or to donate a portion of their allowance and add it to the fish bank each week. When the fish bank is full, send the money to a missionary, along with letters of encouragement.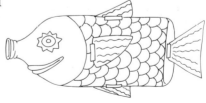

Jesus' Birth

Long ago, a man named Isaiah told people that Jesus would come and help them. Isaiah knew that Jesus is God's Son.

When it was time for Jesus to come, God sent an angel to tell Mary. Mary was afraid at first. She'd never met an angel. But she was happy to hear God had chosen her to be Jesus' mother.

God sent an angel to Joseph in a dream. The angel told Joseph that Mary's baby would be God's Son, Jesus.

Before Jesus was born, Mary and Joseph traveled to Bethlehem. Bethlehem was very crowded. No one had a place for them to stay.

Mary and Joseph had to stay in a stable. Jesus was born there. Mary wrapped him up and laid him in a manger.

Angels appeared to shepherds and told them about Jesus.

The shepherds left their sheep and went to Bethlehem to see Baby Jesus.

Wise men followed a special star to come and worship Jesus. We can worship Jesus, too.

Jesus Christ Is Born

Sing this song to the tune of "The Farmer in the Dell."

Jesus Christ is born!
Jesus Christ is born!
Born today in Bethlehem,
Jesus Christ is born!

Lying in a manger,
Lying in a manger,
Born today in Bethlehem,
Jesus Christ is born!

Glory to God!
Glory to God!
Peace on earth, good will toward men,
Jesus Christ is born!

Baby Jesus

This one is sung to the tune of "Jesus Loves Me."

Baby Jesus, God's own Son,
Born today in Bethlehem.
Horses, donkeys, cows, and sheep
Watched the little baby sleep.

He came to save me.
He came to save you.
He came to save us
Because God loves us so!

Shepherds heard the angels sing,
Then went to see the newborn king.
Later wise men worshiped, too,
Just like you and I should do!

He came to save me.
He came to save you.
He came to save us
Because God loves us so!

Jesus Came

Sing this song to the tune of "Jingle Bells."

Jesus came,
Jesus came,
Jesus came to show
That he's God's Son
And he's the one
God promised long ago.

Jesus came,
Jesus came,
Jesus came to show
That he's God's Son
And he's the one
God promised long ago.

Let's Pray!

Christmas Prayer

Teach children the words and motions to this simple finger play prayer.

**God, thank you for your special
Son** *(pretend to rock a baby),*
**Who came to show that you're
the One!** *(Hold up one finger.)*
He came to wash our sins away
(pretend to wash hands)
**So we can live in heaven some-
day.** *(Point up.)*
Your gift of Jesus helps me see
(point to eyes)
**How much you love and care for
me.** *(Hug self.)*

Thankfulness Gift Wrap

Set out markers, glitter glue, crayons, rubber stamps, ink pads, and a large sheet of newsprint. Have family members think of things they're thankful for, such as a home, school, food, friends, or pets. Allow family members to draw and decorate each praise and say, "Thanks, God, for the gift of…" As you work on your "thankfulness gift wrap," talk about how Jesus is the most special gift God gave us.

EXTRA IDEA! Use your gift wrap to wrap presents for family members who are far away. Not only will they enjoy seeing your children's artwork, they'll love knowing that they're special enough to receive a handmade gift.

New Ways to Pray

✔ Help children remember the wise men's precious gifts to Baby Jesus. Have them pray and thank God for the special "gifts" in their lives, such as health, a family, Jesus, friends, and a safe home.

✔ On a starry night, help children find the brightest star in the sky. Join hands and pray that God will guide them to him each day.

✔ Any time during the year, lead children in singing a Christmas carol such as "Hark! the Herald Angels Sing" or "Joy to the World" as a praise prayer.

Let's Play!

Welcome, Little One

 Just as the wise men celebrated Jesus' birth, your family can join with other families to celebrate the arrival of a baby in your church or neighborhood. Purchase a diaper pail, and fill it with "baby necessities" such as diapers, bottles, a pacifier, blankets, or lotion. (Most of these items can be purchased inexpensively at discount stores.) You might even find items around your home that you're willing to give away, such as clothing, bibs, or crib sheets. Encourage your child to add baby toys that he or she no longer plays with. Tie a bright bow around the diaper pail, and deliver it to welcome the little one.

Heavenly Host

Set out paper muffin cups, tape, glue, and cotton balls. Give each child two muffin cups and a cotton ball. Demonstrate how to fold a muffin cup in half, roll it to make a funnel shape, then tape the edges together. Fold the second muffin cup in half, and tape it to the back of the funnel to form wings. Show children how to glue the cotton ball to the top of the funnel as

the angel's head. Children can make several angels to wear on their fingers, representing the chorus of angels that appeared to the shepherds.

Wise Man, Wise Man

Cut a star from shiny gift wrap. Have children close their eyes while you hide the star. When you've hidden the star, say, "Wise man, wise man, where's your star? You'll need it or you won't get far!" Then allow children to open their eyes and look for the star. You might help them by saying "hot" when they are close to it and "cold" when they move away from it. When one child finds the star, have children close their eyes while he or she hides it.

The Best Gift

Set out graham crackers, frosting, thin licorice whips, and colored sprinkles. Have children break the graham crackers into squares, then frost each square. Show them how to decorate the graham cracker "gifts" with licorice "ribbons." Allow children to add colorful sprinkles for a sparkly touch. As you work, talk about how Baby Jesus was a special gift to us from God.

Five Happy Shepherds

Use this finger play to help children remember the exciting news the shepherds heard.

Five good shepherds watching their sheep. (Hold up five fingers.)
One saw the angel, and up he leaped. (Put other fingers down and hold up only one finger, starting with the thumb.)
"Come," said the angel, "the Savior is here." (Beckon with other hand.)
Away went the shepherd without any fear. (Move hand behind back with thumb still up.)

Repeat the rhyme, holding up four, three, two, then one finger. Finish with this verse:

Five good shepherds standing in a row. (Hold up all five fingers.)
They all found Jesus and bowed down low. (Fold fingers down, making a fist.)
"We love you, Lord Jesus, we love you, we do." (Wiggle fingers excitedly.)
"We'll tell our families and other people, too!"

EXTRA IDEA! Have family members dress up as shepherds. They can use bathrobes, blankets, and towels as costumes; and dowel rods as staffs. Encourage them to act out the rhyme, modifying the number of shepherds to match the number of family members. Talk about ways we can worship Baby Jesus today just as the shepherds did long ago.

You Must Have Been a Beautiful Baby!

Bring out the family photo album, and look at baby pictures of each person in your family. Talk about how surprised and happy you were when you learned that each child was going to be born. Tell children one or two things that were special about each of them at birth.

The Little Lost Sheep

Once there was a shepherd who had 100 sheep. He always took good care of his sheep.

Every day, the shepherd took his sheep to eat grass from the pasture and drink water from the stream.

Every night, the shepherd counted his sheep as they went into the sheepfold.

One night, the shepherd discovered that one of his sheep was missing. He left the other sheep to go look for it.

Finally, the shepherd found his sheep. He pulled it from the bush and carried it home on his shoulders.

The shepherd was so happy that he'd found his sheep! He invited all his friends to come and celebrate with him.

Jesus is like that good shepherd. He'll take care of us and keep us safe, just like the shepherd took care of his sheep.

The Lord Is My Shepherd

 Help children learn Psalm 23:1a with this song, sung to the tune of "The Mulberry Bush."

The Lord is my shepherd *(point up)*,
My shepherd, my shepherd.
(Pretend to hold and pet a lamb.)
The Lord is my shepherd. *(Point up.)*
I shall not want. *(Shake head "no.")*

The Lord is my shepherd *(point up)*,
My shepherd, my shepherd.
(Pretend to hold and pet a lamb.)
The Lord is my shepherd. *(Point up.)*
I shall not want. *(Shake head "no.")*

I'll Talk to the Lord

 This song will help children discover that Jesus, the good shepherd, looks after us even when we're afraid. Sing this song to the tune of "Frère Jacques."

When I'm afraid,
When I'm alone,
I'll talk to the Lord.
I'll talk to the Lord.
I'll tell him how I feel.
I'll tell him how I feel.
He'll help me.
He'll help me.

I'll Follow Jesus

 Use this song, sung to the tune of "Jesus Loves Me," to teach children what it means to follow Jesus.

Jesus loves me this I know,
Where he leads me I will go.
I know he'll take care of me.
He's my shepherd; I'm his sheep.

I'll follow Jesus.
I'll follow Jesus.
I'll follow Jesus.
I'll follow him each day.

 Let's Pray!

A Sheep-ish Prayer

Use this rhyming prayer to help children understand how God is like a shepherd to us.

**Dear God,
The way a shepherd guides his
   sheep,
You guide and love and watch
   o'er me.
Each day please show me the
   right way,
And help me when I want to stray.
Please keep me safe from any
   harm,
And hold me in your loving arms.
Thanks for taking care of me
Just like a shepherd and his
   sheep.**

Protection Prayers

Choose one person to be the "sheep." Have family members form a tight "hug huddle" around the sheep. Pray a prayer similar to this one: **Dear God, thank you for being our shepherd and for loving** (name of family member). **Thank you for your protection and care of** (name) **each day. Help** (name) **be a faithful sheep and follow you in every way. In Jesus' name, amen.**

Allow the sheep to choose a new family member to be the sheep. Pray for each family member.

New Ways to Pray

✔ As you read "The Little Lost Sheep" to children, have them name each of the sheep after someone you know. Pray for your "flock" together, asking God to help them love, follow, and obey God.

✔ Read aloud Psalm 23 from an easy-to-understand translation of the Bible. Pause after each phrase and ask, "How does God do that for us?" Pray after each phrase, thanking God for the specific way he provides for and loves us.

✔ Have children pray and thank God for loving us so much that he found us when we were lost.

 Let's Play!

Sheep in the Fold

 Place a wide-mouthed jar on the floor, and have family members form a circle around it. Distribute cotton ball "sheep," and explain that everyone will try to "shepherd" their sheep into the jar, or "fold." Take turns dropping the cotton balls from chin-height into the jar. (This is one game where small children have an advantage since they're closer to the jar.) See how many sheep you can get into the fold. Talk about how a shepherd takes care of the sheep and gives them a safe place to stay.

Baa-Baa Socks

Give each child an old white sock that's lost its mate. Set out glue, cotton balls, and a few black craft pompoms. Demonstrate how to slip the sock on one arm, then push the toe of the sock between the thumb and fingers to form a puppet. Then dip cotton balls in glue and stick them to the sock to create "fleece" for the sheep puppet. Children will enjoy adding pompom eyes and noses to their puppets.

EXTRA IDEA! When children have finished their puppets, hide a small toy or wrapped treat inside each one. Then hide the sheep puppets, and have children look for them. Talk about how the shepherd looked for his sheep because the sheep was so special to him. Explain that Jesus is our good shepherd and we're very special to him, too.

Sheep Faces

Give each child a small paper plate with a small scoop of vanilla pudding or frozen yogurt on it. Set out raisins, chocolate chips, or shelled peanuts; and help children add eyes, noses, and mouths to their pudding sheep. Encourage children to name their sheep. Remind children that Jesus loves us and knows us by name.

The Shepherd Takes His Sheep

Use this game to teach children that Jesus knows us by name and that we can follow him. Have family members form a circle and hold hands. Lead them in singing "The Shepherd Takes His Sheep" to the tune of "The Farmer in the Dell." Have family members walk around in a circle as you walk around the opposite direction outside the circle. As you call each family member's name, lead him or her out of the circle.

The shepherd takes his sheep.
The shepherd takes his sheep.
Heigh-ho, the derry-o!
The shepherd takes his sheep.

The shepherd takes (name of family member).
The shepherd takes (name of family member).
Heigh-ho, the derry-o!
The shepherd takes (name of family member).

Repeat until all family members are chosen.

The sheep follow him.
The sheep follow him.
Heigh-ho, the derry-o!
The sheep follow him!

Love Lambs

Draw a simple sheep shape on a sheet of paper. Set out cotton balls and glue sticks. Hold up a cotton ball and complete the sentence, "I love you because..." Tell something you love about each child, such as "I love you because you cheer me up when I'm sad" or "I love you because you're a good helper." Then dip the cotton ball in glue, and stick it inside the sheep shape. Allow children to add cotton balls, telling what they love about you and about each other. Continue until you have a fluffy reminder that you're all God's special sheep.

EXTRA IDEA! Use this activity to learn what the Bible says about God's love. Draw a simple sheep shape, and hang it on a refrigerator or bulletin board. Each day have a family member read a verse about God's love, such as John 3:16, Psalm 52:8, or 1 Thessalonians 1:4. Have another family member glue a cotton ball to the sheep shape.

JESUS' MIRACLES

Jesus and Mary went to a wedding party in the town of Cana. The wine ran out, and soon everyone would be thirsty. Mary asked Jesus to help because she knew that Jesus can do anything—and she was right! Jesus turned the water into wine to help his friends.

Jesus and his disciples were sailing
on the Sea of Galilee when a raging
storm came up. The mighty wind tossed the
small boat up and down on the crashing waves.
"Help! Lord, save us!" cried the frightened
disciples.

Jesus raised his arms and faced the raging storm. "Quiet! Be still!" he commanded. At once the wind and waves became calm. Even the wind and water know that Jesus can do anything!

More than 5,000 people listened to Jesus teach about God. The people became hungry, but there was hardly anything to eat. Could Jesus feed so many people with only five loaves of bread and two small fish?

Of course he could! Jesus can do anything. Jesus blessed the food and fed all the hungry people. There were even 12 baskets of leftovers.

One night Jesus walked on the water to be with his disciples in their boat. Peter walked on the water, too, but when he looked away from Jesus he began to sink. Jesus helped Peter back into the boat. Jesus really can do anything!

Jesus Can Do Anything

Sing this song to the tune of "Jesus Loves Me."

**Who can chase my fears away?
Who can turn the night to day?
Who can calm the stormy sea?
Who can grow a mighty tree?**

**Jesus can do anything.
Jesus can do anything.
Jesus can do anything.
There's nothing he can't do!**

I Can Do All Things

Sing this song to the tune of "Old MacDonald."

**I can do all things through Christ
Because he makes me strong.
Jesus helps me do what's right–
He's with me all day long.
He healed the sick,
Fed the crowd.
Everybody shout out loud:
I can do all things through Christ
Because he makes me strong.**

Yes, He Can

This song is sung to the tune of "London Bridge."

Jesus can do anything!
(Hop forward, then hop backward.)
Yes, he can! Clap your hands!
(Clap three times.)
Jesus can do anything!
(Hop forward, then hop backward.)
Yes, he can! *(Twirl around and clap.)*

Jesus can do miracles!
(Hop forward, then hop backward.)
Yes, he can! Clap your hands!
(Clap three times!)
Jesus can do miracles!
(Hop forward, then hop backward.)
Yes, he can! *(Twirl around and clap.)*

Let's Pray!

Powerful God!

Teach children this simple chorus to the tune of "Row, Row, Row Your Boat." Take turns with children, praying for any needs you might have. After each prayer, sing the chorus together to remember that God is mighty enough to help us with our concerns.

God, you're powerful. (Flex muscles.)
In your Word I see (open hands like a book),
You're strong enough. (Flex muscles.)
In you, I trust. (Point up.)
Thanks for loving me. (Hug self.)

Pour Out Your Prayers

Prepare "surprise punch" for your family. Pour a package of presweetened drink mix into a pitcher. Use grape, cherry, or punch-flavored. (It will add to the surprise if the pitcher isn't clear.)

Give each family member a cup of cold water. Explain that Jesus helped his mother at the wedding in Cana. Have family members take turns praying for concerns, such as a sick friend or relative, an upcoming test, a difficult decision, or problems in your community. As family members pray, have them pour their water into the pitcher. When the pitcher is full, say "amen." Stir the punch and explain that we can take our problems to Jesus just as Jesus' mother did. Serve the surprise punch and talk about how sweet it is to talk to Jesus.

New Ways to Pray

✔ One of the greatest miracles is life! With each child, stand in front of a mirror and talk about how miraculous he or she is—from eyes that blink, wink, and cry to hands that clap, snap, and wiggle! Pray and thank God for the miracle of our bodies.

✔ Have children hold heavy bricks or rocks and think of something they need Jesus to do, such as heal a sick friend. Then pray for the concern, and have children set the rocks on the floor. Talk about what it means to give our worries to Jesus.

✔ Link index fingers with your child and thank God for sending Jesus to be our forever friend and Savior.

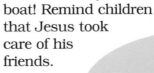

Let's Play!

Swirling Storms

This is a wet craft, best done outside on a hot day.

Set out white card stock and blue or green powdered drink mix. Have children sprinkle some of the drink mix on sheets of paper. Then give children ice cubes and have them rub the ice cubes across their papers. As the ice melts, it will blend with the drink mix to create swirls of color. Talk about the swirling sea that nearly knocked Jesus' friends out of the boat! Remind children that Jesus took care of his friends.

Balloon Sea

 Blow up and tie off about ten blue or green balloons. Call out, "Stormy sea!" and have family members bop the balloons around the room. (Any balloons that pop will only add to the stormy atmosphere!) After about thirty seconds, call out, "Hush! Be still!" Have each person grab several balloons and sit down quietly. Remind family members that Jesus spoke and calmed a real storm.

EXTRA IDEA! End this game with a reminder of how Peter walked on the water. Spread the balloons across the floor to create a "lake." Then have family members "walk on the water" and pop the balloons.

The Miracle Basket

 Use a laundry basket to help children review the miracles Jesus performed.

● To portray the miracle at Cana, have children pretend that the laundry basket is a jug of water. Tell the story, and have children "pour wine" from the jug. Talk about how surprised everyone was!

● Have your child sit in the basket, rock back and forth, and pretend to be a disciple on the stormy sea. Tell how Jesus calmed the sea, and have your child "calm" the laundry-basket boat. Then talk about how Peter walked on the water to Jesus. Have your child step out of the basket and pretend to walk on wind-blown waves.

● Help children weave colorful crepe paper streamers through the open squares of the laundry basket. (You can fold the strips of crepe paper in half so they'll go through the open squares of the basket more easily.) As you work, talk about the baskets of food that were left over from one little boy's lunch.

Banana Boats

 Give each child a banana and thirteen chocolate chips or raisins. Demonstrate how to peel away one strip of the banana peel. Have each child scoop out a little of the center portion of the banana and then put the chocolate chips or raisins in the scooped-out part. Talk about how Jesus helped his friends when they were afraid and he helped Peter step out of the boat and onto the water!

Love That Grows

 Thaw a loaf of frozen bread dough. Have each child shape a handful of the dough into a heart-shaped loaf. As you work, talk about the loaves of bread that the boy gave to Jesus. Remind children that the little loaves fed thousands of hungry people!

Place the loaves on a greased baking sheet, cover with a towel, and set in a warm place for about a half-hour. When you check the loaves again, point out how much they've "grown." Place them in the oven and bake according to package directions. Talk about how God's love for us grows, too. Point out that just as Jesus didn't run out of food for the hungry people, God never runs out of love for us.

EXTRA IDEA! Just as the little boy shared his lunch, children can share this special snack with someone. Have children wrap each heart-shaped loaf in colorful tissue paper. Place each loaf in a gift basket with a small jar of favorite jam or honey. Have children draw gift tags for the baskets, being sure to keep their identities hidden! Children can help you secretly deliver the gifts.

A Bunch of Lunch

 To remind children of the "picnic" that Jesus provided for five thousand people, have children pack a picnic lunch for two or three friends. Help children make sandwiches, choose fruit, pour drinks into thermos bottles, and find other fun and nutritious snacks to add. As you work together, ask children, "How much lunch do you think we'll need?" Talk about how Jesus made a little tiny lunch go a long, long way!

The Miracle of Easter

One day Jesus told two of his disciples to go into town and find a young donkey that was tied up. Jesus said, "Bring the colt to me. If anyone asks you why you are taking it, say, 'The Master needs it.'" The two disciples found the donkey and brought it to Jesus.

The disciples put their coats on the donkey's back to make it soft for Jesus to ride on. When Jesus rode the donkey into Jerusalem, a huge crowd gathered to greet him. Some people spread their coats and palm branches on the road. Everyone waved and cheered, "Hosanna! Blessed is he who comes in the name of the Lord."

Jesus sent two of his friends to prepare the special Passover meal. That night Jesus shared his last meal with his disciples. Jesus gave thanks for the bread and the cup and shared them with his friends. He asked his friends to remember him whenever they ate this special meal.

After the Passover meal, Jesus and his friends went to a garden to pray. Jesus was sad and troubled, so he asked God to help him. Jesus wanted his friends to pray with him, but they fell asleep. Later that night, soldiers came and took Jesus away.

Jesus had never done anything wrong. But mean people told lies about Jesus and said Jesus had done lots of bad things. So they hung Jesus on a cross to die. All of Jesus' friends were sad and scared. They didn't understand that Jesus died on the cross to take the punishment for all the wrong things people do.

On Sunday morning, three women went to the tomb to take care of Jesus' body. They worried about how to roll the big stone away. But when they got to the tomb, the stone was already rolled away! A bright, shining angel showed them the empty tomb and said that Jesus was alive!

Many people saw Jesus after he rose from the dead. Jesus told his followers to travel everywhere and tell everyone that he was alive again. Jesus said, "I am with you always." Soon afterward, Jesus rose into the clouds and went back to heaven to be with God. Someday, we'll live with Jesus in heaven, too.

Jesus is alive today! He loves us and wants us to celebrate the new life that he gives us. Hallelujah! Jesus is alive!

Let's All Sing

 Your family can celebrate the joy of Palm Sunday any time of the year with this song, sung to the tune of "Old MacDonald."

**Let's all sing and praise the Lord.
Ho-ho-hosanna!
Jesus lives forevermore.
Ho-ho-hosanna!**

**He's the Son of God,
Who showed his love.
Praise to God in heav'n above!
Let's all sing and praise the Lord.
Ho-ho-hosanna!**

I'll Remember

 This song will help children understand the importance of remembering that Jesus died for our sins and rose again. Sing it to the tune of "Jesus Loves Me."

**Jesus said, "Remember me,"
Then he died for you and me.
I know Jesus is God's Son.
I'll remember what he's done.**

Yes, I'll remember.
(Nod and tap temple.)
Yes, I'll remember.
(Nod and tap temple.)
Yes, I'll remember *(nod and tap temple)*
That Jesus died for me. *(Touch middle finger of right hand to palm of left hand, then vice versa to sign "Jesus," then point to self.)*

**Jesus is alive today.
He rose again on the third day.
He watches me from heav'n above.
I'll remember his great love.**

Yes, I'll remember.
(Nod and tap temple.)
Yes, I'll remember.
(Nod and tap temple.)
Yes, I'll remember *(nod and tap temple)*
That Jesus is alive. *(Touch opposite palms with middle fingers to sign "Jesus.")*

Jesus Gives New Life

 Teach children this song to help them realize that Jesus' death and resurrection changes our lives forever! Sing this song to the tune of "This Old Man."

Jesus came. *(Clap three times.)*
Praise his name! *(Clap three times.)*
I will never be the same.
(Shake head from side to side.)
Jesus died to take my sins away.
(Hold arms out to form a cross, then pretend to toss something away.)
Jesus gives new life today. *(Point up, then cross arms on chest.)*

Celebrate! *(Wave hands in the air.)*
Celebrate! *(Wave hands in the air.)*
Thank God for this special date!
(Clap seven times.)
Jesus rose again on Easter day.
(Raise arms with palms up.)
Jesus gives new life today. *(Point up, then cross arms on chest.)*

Let's Pray!

Hosanna Praise Palms

Give each family member a sheet of green construction paper, a marker, and a twelve-inch strip of poster board. Explain that when Jesus rode into Jerusalem, people praised him and said nice things about him. Point out that we can praise God, too. Have family members trace at least two sets of their hands on green construction paper and cut out the hand prints.

Then have each person write or draw praises on each hand print. Family members might write things such as "Jesus died and rose again!" or "God cares for each of us." Or they can draw pictures of hearts, birds, or things God created. Then have family members tape their hand prints to the poster board strips to create palm fronds. Hold a praise prayer parade by playing upbeat music, waving your palm fronds, and calling out your praises!

Tell Me More About God

Use this simple song as a reminder of the many words that describe God. Sing it to the tune of "God Is So Good." Encourage your children to fill in the blanks with words such as "powerful," "loving," or "beautiful."

God, you're so _____.
God, you're so _____.
God, you're so _____.
                I will follow you.

New Ways to Pray

✔ Have family members rub their hands with newspaper while silently confessing their sins. Then pray for each other while washing each other's hands. Encourage children to thank God for sending Jesus to wash away our sins.

✔ Pray with children and praise God for being mighty enough to defeat death. Close your prayer by giving high fives!

✔ Help children think of friends, family members, neighbors, teachers, and others who don't know the good news of God's love. Pray for those people and ask God to help your family share his message.

Let's Play!

Easter Spices

Help each child cut a four-by-six-inch cross from rough sandpaper. Set out whole cinnamon sticks, and demonstrate how to rub the cinnamon over the sandpaper cross. Punch a hole

in the top of the cross and string a length of ribbon through it to make a hanger. Explain that when the women went to the tomb, they took sweet-smelling spices to put on Jesus' body. Remind children that when the women got to the tomb, they discovered that Jesus had risen from the dead!

EXTRA IDEA! Children can add additional spices and color to their crosses. Allow children to decorate the sandpaper crosses with glitter glue, then help them sprinkle spices such as ginger, nutmeg, allspice, or ground cloves on the wet glue.

Rockin' and Rollin'

 Play this game outside, or clear the furniture out of the way if you play inside. Have family members line up at one end of the playing area. Instruct the first person in line to lie on the ground and roll across the playing area, then stand up and run back to the line. (It won't be easy to run because players will be dizzy!) Continue playing until everyone has had a turn. Talk about how the heavy stone was rolled away from Jesus' tomb.

Resurrection Biscuits

 Set out large marshmallows, refrigerator biscuit dough, a bowl of melted margarine, and a bowl of cinnamon sugar. Have children flatten the uncooked biscuits, wrap a marshmallow in each one, and pinch the edges tightly together. Then help children dip the dough balls into melted margarine and roll them in cinnamon sugar. Bake the biscuits at 375 degrees for about ten minutes or until they're lightly browned. When the biscuits are cool, give one to each family member. They'll get a big surprise when they bite into the treats. They'll be hollow and empty, just like the tomb!

A Special Meal

 Help children plan a special meal, featuring their favorite foods. Allow children to help prepare the meal by doing tasks such as stirring batter, tearing lettuce for a salad, or filling a pitcher with ice water. As you work together, talk about the special meal that Jesus shared with his friends. Explain that Jesus wanted his friends to remember him whenever they ate that special meal. During your meal, have family members share memorable family moments, such as fun vacations or silly birthday gifts. Close your meal by praying and thanking God for your family.

New Life

 Purchase several terra cotta planters. Help children cut cross shapes from sponges, then sponge-paint crosses on each planter. Spoon in potting soil, have children drop in a few marigold seeds, and cover the seeds with a thin layer of soil. Remind children to water the seeds frequently and keep them on a sunny windowsill. When the seeds begin to sprout, give the plants away as bright reminders of the new life Jesus gives us.

A Forever Friend

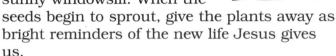 Use this action rhyme to teach children that Jesus died for our sins and rose again. Explain that the last motion is the sign for "friend."

Jesus died upon a cross (stretch out arms and bow head)
To take our sins away. (Hug self.)
Jesus' friends were sad to see (rub eyes)
Their Savior die that day.
But now we all can celebrate (wiggle fingers),
For Jesus rose again. (Keep wiggling fingers, raise hands.)
So we can live in heaven (point up)
With Jesus as our friend! (Link index fingers together.)

EXTRA IDEA! From your local library, get a book on sign language for children. Teach children signs to help them discover new ways to communicate the good news about Jesus.

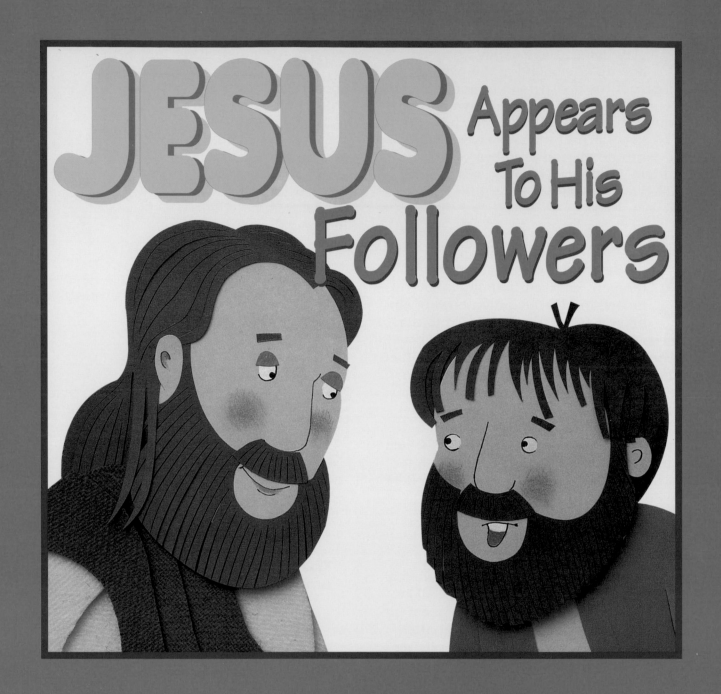

A few days after Jesus died, two of his friends went for a walk. They were very sad. They missed Jesus.

As Jesus' friends were walking, another man joined them. They told the man how much they missed Jesus.

They asked the man to have dinner with them. The man gave thanks for the food and passed it out to everyone. They realized he was Jesus!

The two friends hurried to Jerusalem to tell Jesus' other friends that they'd seen Jesus. While they were talking about how they met Jesus, Jesus appeared again! Jesus' friends were so excited to see him. They told their friend Thomas that Jesus was alive. But Thomas wouldn't believe them.

Later Jesus appeared again. This time Thomas was there, too. When Thomas saw Jesus' hands, he finally believed Jesus was alive.

Jesus asked his friends to go everywhere and tell people that he was alive. Then he went back to heaven to be with God.

Later, when Jesus' friends met together, flames of fire appeared, but the flames didn't burn them. Everyone was filled with the Holy Spirit. The Holy Spirit is a special helper Jesus sends to his friends on earth. The Holy Spirit helped Jesus' friends tell others about Jesus. The Holy Spirit can help us tell others about Jesus, too.

Spread the Good News

Use this song to get your children excited about telling others about Jesus. This song is sung to the tune of "Old MacDonald."

Spread the good news everywhere.
(Hold arms up, and turn in a circle.)
Jesus is alive! *(Pat hands against a partner's hands.)*
Take the good news here and there. *(Point around the room.)*
Jesus is alive! *(Pat hands against partner's.)*
Step-step-hop. *(Step, step, hop.)*
Don't be slow. *(Wave "come on.")*
Right foot, left foot *(step with right foot, then left foot),*
Do-si-do! *(Cross arms over chest, then circle around partner.)*
Spread the good news everywhere.
(Hold arms up, and turn in a circle.)
Jesus is alive! *(Pat hands against a partner's.)*

I Believe

Sing this song with your children to help them express their faith in Jesus. Sing it to the tune of "Frère Jacques."

I believe.
I believe.
Yes, I do.
Yes, I do!
I believe in Jesus.
I believe in Jesus.
You can, too.
You can, too!

G–I–V–E

This song will teach your children simple ways to follow Jesus and tell others about him. Sing this song to the tune of "Old MacDonald."

Put the g–i–v–e back
Into the word "forgive."
That's the way my Jesus wants
M–e, me, to live.
I will care.
I will share.
Spread his love
Everywhere!
Put the g–i–v–e back
Into the word "forgive."

Let's Pray!

Casting Our Cares

Use this song to help children learn to give their problems to God. Sing the song to the tune of "Frère Jacques," then pray about any problems or concerns children might have.

**I give my problems,
I give my problems
To you, Lord,
To you, Lord–
For I know that you love me
And that you'll take care of me.
Amen,
Amen.**

Prayer Gloves

Purchase inexpensive pairs of cotton knit gloves for your children. Have them put the gloves on, then talk about how Thomas wouldn't believe that Jesus was alive until he saw Jesus' hands. Explain that we can show we believe in Jesus by praying. Help children draw small pictures of friends, teachers, neighbors, and family members. Tape a picture to each finger of the gloves. Have children hold up their fingers, one by one, and pray for each person. You can also use the prayer gloves for giving thanks. Cut out pictures of things children are thankful for, and tape them to the fingers of the gloves. Children can give thanks for each blessing.

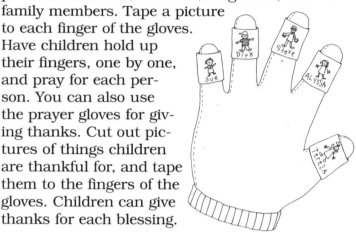

New Ways to Pray

✔ Draw a red dot on the hand of each family member. Stand in a circle and silently pray, confessing any wrongdoing. Then use soapy water to scrub the dots away. Have your family huddle for a group hug and thank Jesus for taking our sins away.

✔ Choose a grassy area for your family to lie in and look up at the sky. Talk about the place Jesus went to prepare for those who believe in him and love him. Pray and thank God for loving us enough to spend eternity with us.

✔ Join children in praying for a world of doubting Thomases. Ask God to reveal ways to show Jesus to an unbelieving world.

Let's Play!

Pentecost Windsocks

 Set out red, yellow, and orange crepe paper; red, yellow, and orange crayons; scissors; glue sticks; string; and tape. Give children paper lunch

sacks, and help them cut the bottom out of the bags. Have children color their bags, then help them cut strips of crepe paper to glue onto the end of the bags. When the glue has dried, help them each tape a piece of string onto one end of the bag as a handle. As you work, talk about what it might have been like to hear "a noise like a strong, blowing wind" and see "something like flames of fire" when the Holy Spirit came.

I Spy Jesus

 Play a game of I Spy with your family. Take turns giving clues about an item in the room. Use clues such as "I spy something yellow. It gives light in the dark room. What do I spy?" Family members have three tries to guess the item.

Point out that even though we don't "spy" Jesus with our eyes, we can believe in him.

EXTRA IDEA! Encourage children to look for examples of Jesus every day. Whenever children see someone being kind, sharing, helping, or listening, have them say, "I spy Jesus!" Talk about how we can be like Jesus to people who don't know him.

Into the Clouds

 Sit outside, and take turns blowing bubbles with children. Each time you blow bubbles, tell one thing you're looking forward to seeing in heaven. You might mention things such as "I'm looking forward to seeing grandma" or "I can't wait to give Jesus a hug." As you watch the bubbles rise, talk about Jesus' ascension and that he went to heaven to prepare a place for each of us. Remind children that Jesus loves us so much that he wants us to be in heaven with him forever.

Not by Sight

 Give children unpeeled oranges. As children hold and smell the oranges, talk about what's inside the orange peel. Ask children how they know that there's an orange inside the peel. Explain that even though we can't see the orange, we know that it's inside the peel. Point out that even though we can't see Jesus, we can believe in him. Talk about ways we can show others that we believe in Jesus, such as sharing, telling Bible stories, singing songs about Jesus, and loving others.

Surprise Cookies

 Make or purchase sugar-cookie dough. Set out a bowl of chocolate mints, and show children how to roll a chocolate mint into a ball of cookie dough. When children have used up all the dough, bake the cookies according to

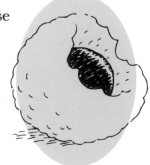

package directions. While the cookies bake, talk about how surprised your family members will be when they find a surprise inside their cookies! Remind children that Jesus' friends were very surprised when they recognized Jesus and realized that he was alive. When the cookies have cooled, children can share the surprise with family members!

Jesus Is Alive!

 Use this action rhyme to teach children the exciting events that happened after Jesus died and rose again.

When Jesus' time on earth was through (*use hands to form a circle to indicate "earth"*),
He told his good friends what to do:
"Travel here and travel there (*walk in place*)
And tell about me everywhere."
(*Hold arms out wide to indicate "everywhere."*)

Then Jesus rose up in the sky.
(*Point up.*)
His friends all watched him rise up high.
Just when a cloud hid him from sight (*look around*),
They saw two angels shining white. (*Open fingers quickly to indicate "shining."*)

And when they met on Pentecost day (*sit down*),
God sent a Special Friend their way. (*Point up.*)
The Holy Spirit came right down (*flutter hands down like a dove*)
And helped them spread the word around. (*Cup hands to mouth and pretend to talk to someone.*)

Jesus is alive today! (*Clap hands.*)
Listen now to what we say. (*Cup hands to ear as if listening.*)
If you believe in him and pray (*fold hands in prayer*),
He will take your sins away. (*Cross arms over chest.*)

SAUL'S SURPRISE
ON THE ROAD TO DAMASCUS

Saul did not like the followers of Jesus! He did everything he could to make them stop telling people that Jesus was God's Son. Saul arrested Christians, threw them in prison, and sometimes even had them killed! But the church kept growing! So one day, Saul went to the high priest and got permission to arrest any Christians he could find in the city of Damascus.

Saul and his helpers set off for Damascus. Just before they reached the city, a blinding light from heaven flashed, and Saul fell to the ground. Saul heard the voice of Jesus ask, "Saul, Saul, why do you keep trying to hurt me?" Then Jesus' voice told Saul to go to Damascus and wait to be told what to do. When Saul got up to obey, he couldn't see anything! He was blind. So Saul's friends led him to Damascus, where he waited and prayed for three days.

God spoke to a church leader named Ananias and told him to heal Saul of his blindness. But Ananias was afraid to meet Saul. He knew that Saul was in Damascus to arrest Jesus' followers. But God assured Ananias that Saul would spread the good news about Jesus to kings and people of many nations.

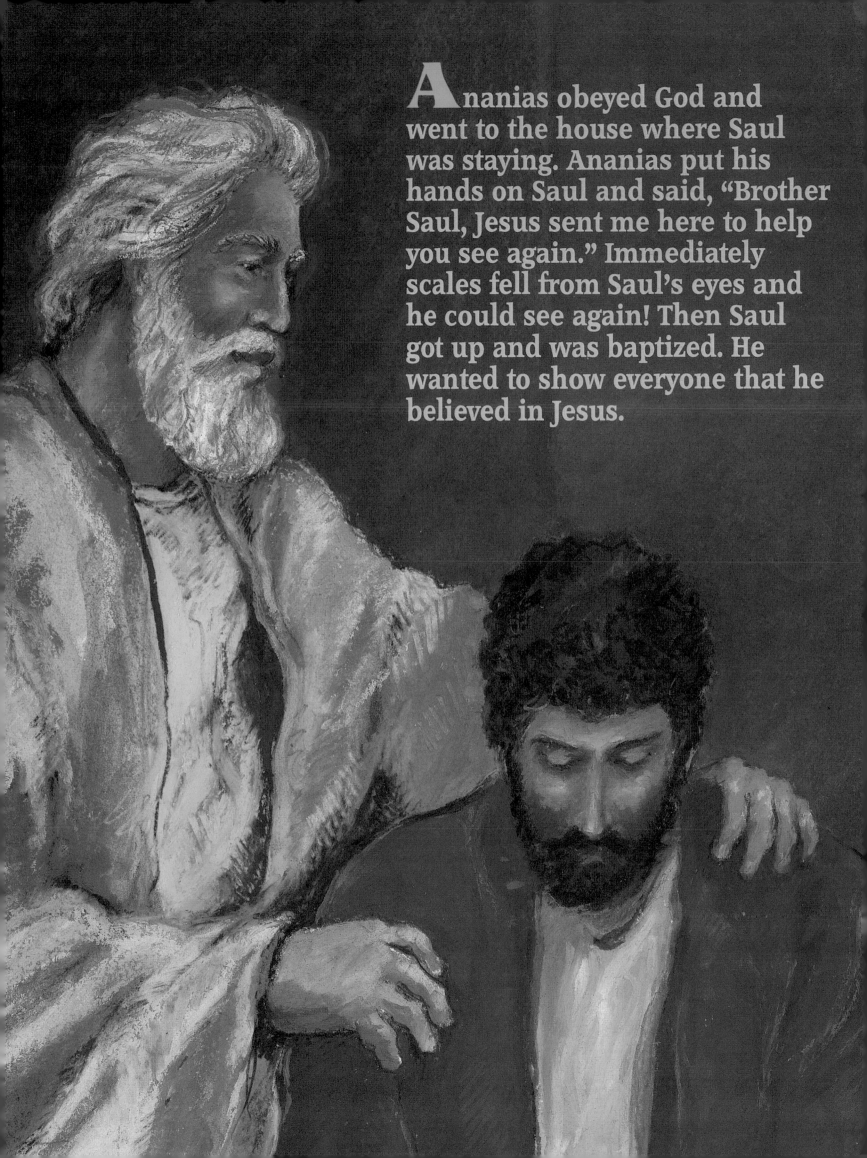

Ananias obeyed God and went to the house where Saul was staying. Ananias put his hands on Saul and said, "Brother Saul, Jesus sent me here to help you see again." Immediately scales fell from Saul's eyes and he could see again! Then Saul got up and was baptized. He wanted to show everyone that he believed in Jesus.

Instead of arresting the Christians in Damascus, Saul became friends with them. In fact, he began preaching in the synagogue, telling everyone that Jesus was the Son of God. He was such a good preacher that no one could argue with him. Everyone who heard Saul was amazed. "Is this really the same man who came here to arrest Jesus' followers?" people asked.

But not everyone was happy about the change in Saul. Saul's old friends who didn't believe in Jesus decided to kill Saul because he wasn't on their side anymore. But Saul heard of their plans. Then Saul's friends in the church came up with a plan of their own. In the dark of night, they lowered Saul in a large basket through an opening in the city wall. Because of their help, Saul escaped.

When Saul got back to Jerusalem, the Christians there were afraid of him. How could they trust the man who used to be their enemy? Only Barnabas believed Saul. Barnabas helped everyone see that Saul was truly a follower of Jesus. Soon Saul began preaching about Jesus in Jerusalem. Then he traveled far and wide, teaching people in many different countries about God's Son, Jesus.

Loving God

Use these words to teach your children 1 John 5:3a. Sing this song to the tune of "Ten Little Indians."

Loving God means obeying his commands.
Loving God means obeying his commands.
Loving God means obeying his commands.
First John five three a.

Let's Give

Sing this song to teach your children some of the ways to help others. Sing it to the tune of "The Farmer in the Dell."

Let's give a helping hand (wiggle fingers)
To anyone we can. (Point around the room.)
Here's my right hand (raise right hand),
Here's my left (raise left hand),
Let's give a helping hand. (Wiggle fingers.)

Let's give a kind word, too (move hands like a puppet mouth),
When our friends feel blue. (Make a sad face.)
A kind word always shows we care. (Hug self.)
Let's give a kind word, too. (Move hands like a puppet mouth.)

Let's give with hearts of love (make a heart shape on chest with pointer fingers)
Good news from God above.
(Point up.)
Jesus came to save us all.
(Put arms around each other.)
Let's give with hearts of love. (Make a heart shape on chest with pointer fingers.)

God Calls Us

Play a game of Follow the Leader as you teach children this song to the tune of "Old MacDonald." This song reinforces the importance of following and obeying God every day.

God calls us to follow him
Every single day!
God calls us to follow him.
He'll lead us all the way.

Follow God!
He loves you, too!
Do just what he says to do.

God calls us to follow him
Every single day!

God calls us to obey him
Every single day!
God calls us to obey him.
He wants us to obey.

Obey God!
He loves you, too!
Do just what he says to do.

God calls us to obey him
Every single day!

Let's Pray!

Take All of Me

Lead children in this finger play prayer to teach them that God can use us to tell others the good news.

Lord, help me use my voice to say
(touch lips)
Kind words to people every day.
(Pat someone on the back.)
Lord, use my hands–although they're small *(hold up hands)*—
To show your love to one and all.
(Hug someone.)
Lord, use my feet to take your word *(walk in place)*
To people who might not have heard. *(Put hand to ear.)*
Use all of me to share the news
(outstretch arms)
So others can love you as I do!
(Point up, then to self.)

Helping Feet

Roll out a six-foot length of butcher paper or newspaper for each child. Pour washable tempera paint into a pie tin, and add a few drops of liquid soap for easy cleanup. Have children take off their shoes and socks, step into the pie tin, and walk across the paper. (You'll probably need to help wash children's feet!) While the paint dries, talk about all the places Paul went, telling people about Jesus. Have children draw pictures next to the footprints of places where they can tell people about Jesus. Children might draw pictures of a school, a park, grandma's house, or a swimming pool. Hang a footprint poster in each child's room and lead him or her in praying for the people at those places each day.

New Ways to Pray

✔ Have children pray and ask God to help them be "Barnabas buddies" to those who need encouragement.

✔ To remember how Saul's friends helped him, have family members take turns standing or sitting in a laundry basket. Allow the person in the basket to share specific prayer requests, such as an upcoming test, safety for a business trip, or the courage to share Jesus with a friend. Then take turns praying for the person in the basket.

✔ Show children the picture of Ananias from "Saul's Surprise: On the Road to Damascus." Talk about some hard things that God asks us to do, such as being kind, sharing, or loving people who are mean. Pray and ask God to help you follow his instructions, just as Ananias did.

Let's Play!

Out–a–Sight Snacks

Set out large twisted pretzels and long red licorice whips. Show children how to weave the licorice between the pretzels and then pull the ends out to make silly glasses. Children may want to wear their glasses before eating them! Talk about how Ananias prayed for Saul so that Saul could see again.

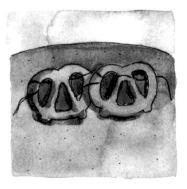

Bright Lights

 Have children color index cards with brightly colored crayons, such as yellow, orange, and red. Be sure the cards are filled with color! Then have children scribble heavily over their cards with black crayons. When the cards are covered with black crayon, show children how to straighten paper clips and use the pointy ends to scrape off the black crayon, revealing the bright colors underneath. Children might draw pictures of bright lights, such as fireworks, stars, or the sun. Remind children that Saul saw a bright light, then became blind.

Sing and Follow Jesus

 Talk about how Saul's life changed when he decided to follow Jesus. Then ask children how our lives are different when we follow Jesus. Have family members form a circle and then sing and play this game. Sing the song to the tune of the "Hokey Pokey."

You put your right hand in (put your right hand in the circle),
You put your right hand out (put your right hand outside the circle),
You put your right hand in and you shake it all about. (Put your hand into the middle of the circle and shake it.)
You want to follow Jesus, so you turn your life around. (Turn around in a circle.)
That's what it's all about! (Clap on each word.)

Repeat the song, substituting the following words in each verse: **left hand, right leg, left leg, head,** and **whole self.**

Balloon Blessings

 Talk about how Barnabas encouraged Saul, then explain that God wants us to encourage each other, too. Have each family member write his or her name on an uninflated balloon, then exchange balloons. Instruct each person to give a word of encouragement to the person whose name is written on the balloon, then blow into the balloon. Take turns encouraging each other and blowing up the balloons. Everyone will see how kind words build people up! Tie off the balloons and hang them up as reminders to encourage each other.

Follow and Obey

 Hide a Bible in your home. Mark 1 John 5:3a with the end of a ball of yarn, then run the yarn all over the house and even outside! Give your child the end of the yarn and have him or her roll the yarn, following it to the Bible. Read the verse and talk about how Saul showed his love for God by obeying.

EXTRA IDEA! Use this same game to help children learn the Ten Commandments. Each time you play, talk about the importance of learning and following God's rules.

Lend-a-Hand Basket

 Place a plastic strawberry basket on the table, and give each person a pencil and two or three strips of colored paper. Have family members write ways they can help others just as Saul's friends helped him. Family members might think of ideas such as weeding a friend's lawn, fixing a meal for a sick neighbor, washing windows for an elderly church member, or baby-sitting for another family. Place the paper strips in the basket, and allow a different family member to take one and read it each week. Commit to following the action that week.

HELP GRANDMA WEED HER GARDEN

EXTRA IDEA! If your family runs out of ideas, call your church secretary for information about needs in your church or community. And keep your eyes open for community fliers or ads in your local paper that tell about community charity events.

Paul and Silas were best friends. They traveled together from city to city, telling people about Jesus. One day Paul and Silas helped a slave girl who had a bad spirit inside her. The slave girl's owners got very angry. They grabbed Paul and Silas and dragged them away.

Paul and Silas stood before the city leaders. The slave girl's owners said, "These men are making trouble in our city!" Soon a crowd of people joined the angry men. They hit Paul and Silas with sticks and tore their clothes. Then they threw Paul and Silas in jail.

The jail guards put heavy chains on Paul and Silas and locked their feet in between big blocks of wood. The guards wanted to make sure Paul and Silas couldn't escape. One of the jailers watched them very carefully. It was his job to make sure they didn't get away.

The jail cell was dark and dirty. Paul and Silas felt sore and hungry. But instead of being afraid or crying or getting mad, Paul and Silas started singing to God! They prayed and talked to God, too. Late into the night, as Paul and Silas sang and prayed, the other prisoners listened. They could hardly believe their ears!

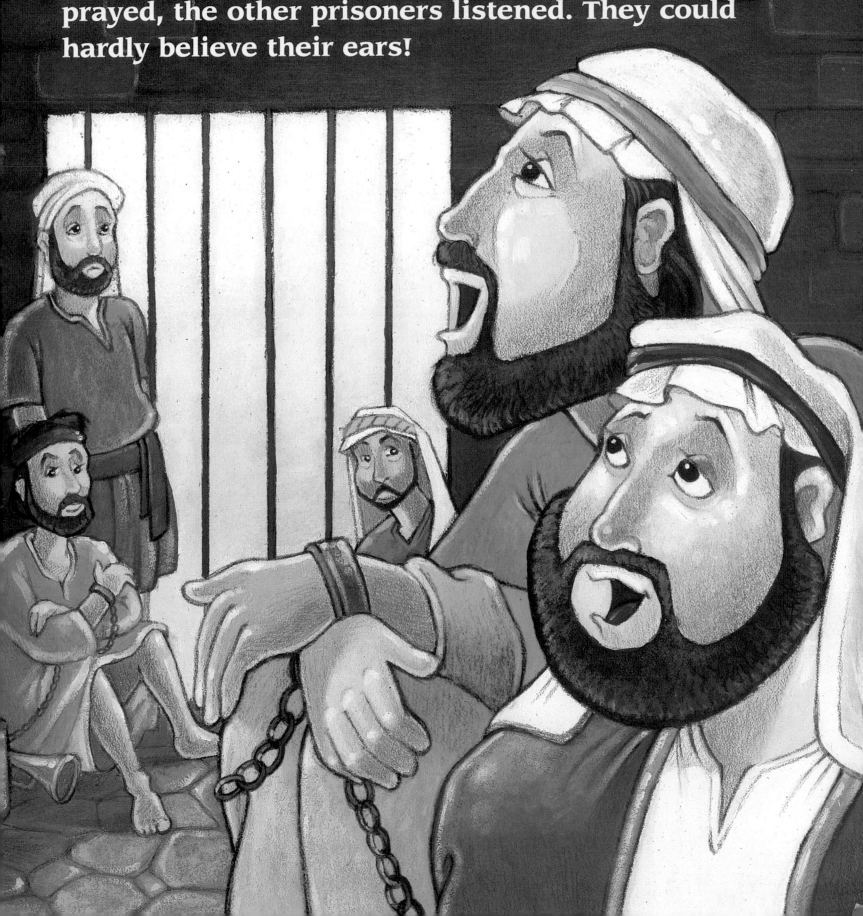

Suddenly the ground began to shake, and the floor began to quake! It was an earthquake! The prison doors broke open! The prisoners' chains fell off! When the jailer heard all the noise and saw the open doors, he thought, "Oh, no! Everyone will escape, and I'll be in big trouble!" He grabbed a sword to kill himself. But Paul shouted, "Don't hurt yourself! We're all here."

The jailer looked around. It was true! Everyone was still there. He fell to his knees and asked, "What must I do to be saved?" Paul said, "Believe in the Lord Jesus." The jailer took Paul and Silas to his home. He washed their sores and fed them dinner. Then Paul and Silas told the jailer's family all about Jesus.

A Joyful Noise

Use this worship song to lead children in praising God. This song is sung to the tune of "Did You Ever See a Lassie?"

We are glad to make a joyful noise,
Joyful noise, joyful noise.
Let's all make a joyful noise
Unto the Lord.
Let's clap and sing. (Clap.)
Let's dance and praise him. (Wave hands in the air, and twirl around.)
We are glad to make a joyful noise
Unto the Lord.

We Help Others

Teach your children this song to help them discover ways to show God's love. Sing it to the tune of "Ten Little Indians."

With the good words that we say
(make your hands "talk")
And our kind actions as we play
(shake hands with someone),
We can show God's love each day
(hug self)
And help others learn about God.
(Point up.)

We've come to church to sing and pray. (Fold hands in prayer.)
We'll listen to God's Word today
(cup hands around ears),
Then pass on what we've learned—hooray! (Pretend to whisper to a friend, then jump up.)
We'll help others learn about God.
(Point up.)

God Wants Me

Sing this song with children to teach them that we can be like Paul and Silas and tell people about God. Sing it to the tune of "This Old Man."

God wants me (point to self),
God wants you (point to partner)
To go and share the happy news.
(Join hands, and walk in a circle.)
Jesus came to show us all God's love (touch middle finger of right hand to palm of left hand, then vice versa, then hug self)
And point the way to heaven above. (Point up.)

Near and far (pat partner's hands, then clap),
Here and there (point to another pair, then point to self),
God loves people everywhere!
(Turn around in a circle.)
Let's all go and tell about God's love (join hands and walk in a circle)
And point the way to heaven above! (Point up.)

Let's Pray!

Prayer Chain

Help children write or draw prayer requests on two-by-eight-inch strips of construction paper. Children might have concerns such as a sick relative, moving to a new home or school, safety, or a friend who doesn't know Jesus. When you've written at least ten prayer requests, show children how make prayer chains by gluing the strips into links and looping them together, as shown. Each day join children in praying for one of the concerns, and "breaking the chain" by tearing that link.

Mighty God

Teach children this praise prayer to the tune of "Old MacDonald." Each time you sing it, encourage children to fill in new words that describe God, such as awesome, gentle, holy, and Father.

**You, O Lord, are powerful.
I've seen what you can do!
But even though you're mighty strong,
You're kind and loving, too!**

**You help me out
When I'm in need.
Thank you, God, for loving me!**

**You, O Lord, are powerful.
I've seen what you can do!**

New Ways to Pray

✔ Encourage compassion in children by praying together for people who are in prison. Be sure to thank God for loving all of us even when we do wrong things.

✔ As you read the story of "Paul and Silas Go to Jail," help children find the horns hidden on each page. Each time a child finds a horn, sing a simple praise song as a prayer. Explain that singing is a super way to tell God how much we love him.

✔ Paul and Silas went through many hard times. Pray with your family for someone who is going through a difficult time. Ask God to help that person through the difficulty and to show your family how to be encouragers.

Let's Play!

Jailhouse Snacks

Help each child spread peanut butter or marshmallow creme on graham crackers. Place two gummy bears on the peanut butter to represent Paul

and Silas. Then have children place thin, black licorice whips vertically across the graham crackers to make "jail bars." While you're enjoying your snacks, talk about how Paul and Silas praised God even while they were in jail!

Earthquake Shakers

Set out crayons, markers, paper plates, and bowls of dry pasta. Have each family member decorate one side of a paper plate, then show them how to fold their plates in half so the decorated side is on the outside. Instruct each person to pour a spoonful of pasta into each folded plate and then staple around the edges. Use the "earthquake shakers" to accompany your family while you sing praise songs together.

EXTRA IDEA! Children can make more earthquake shakers by pouring spoonfuls of dry beans, rice, or pasta into clean, empty yogurt containers. Glue or tape the lids on, and children can shake and quake away!

Earthshaking Experience!

Have family members stand around an old blanket or sheet, then choose one family member to sit in the middle of the blanket. When you say, "Earthquake coming!" have everyone pick up the edge of the blanket and shake it back and forth, jiggling the rider. Then call, "Jailbreak!" and have the "earthquake" stop so the person in the middle can jump up and choose another family member to be in the middle.

Love Bandages

Set out crayons and fifteen-inch strips of white crepe paper streamers or paper towel strips. Work with children and draw bright designs on the streamers. You might draw things such as happy faces, stars, hearts, suns, and flowers. Explain that these streamers look like bandages that would be used to cover cuts and scrapes. Remind children that the jailer washed and bandaged Paul's and Silas' sores to show that he was thankful to hear about Jesus. Take turns wrapping the "love bandages" around each other's arms or legs. Talk about how we're wrapped in God's love.

Cheerful Worship

Remind children that Paul and Silas sang praise songs even when they were in jail. Help children choose four or five favorite praise songs. Then place a blank cassette into a cassette recorder, and join children in singing each song into the recorder. Be sure to allow children to add a few praise phrases such as "God is great!" or "I love Jesus!" between each song. Send your praise tape to a relative or college student who's far from home.

Prison Praises

Set up a pretend jail by taping black crepe paper "jail bars" to the edge of a table. Have your family crowd into the jail and listen while you read the story "Paul and Silas Go to Jail." When the story ends, sing a praise song together and tear down the jail bars. Roll out from the jail and tell each other the good news about Jesus.

EXTRA IDEA! Choose one family member to be the "jailer." Have the jailer send each person to jail by saying things such as "If you're wearing white socks, you have to go to jail" or "If you have two arms, you have to go to jail." When everyone is in jail, talk about how Paul and Silas were sent to jail even though they didn't do anything wrong.

Evaluation of *Pray & Play Bible for Young Children*

Please help Group Publishing continue to provide innovative and usable resources for ministry by taking a moment to fill out and send us this evaluation. Thanks!

• • •

1. As a whole, this book has been (circle one):

Not much help   Very helpful

1   2   3   4   5   6   7   8   9   10

2. The things I liked best about this book were:

3. This book could be improved by:

4. One thing I'll do differently because of this book is:

5. Optional Information:

Name _____

Street Address _____

City _____ State _____ Zip _____

Phone Number _____ Date _____

37 fun songs!

Enjoy these fun songs that help your child remember favorite stories from the *Pray & Play Bible for Young Children!*

Here are 37 upbeat *Pray & Play Songs for Young Children* — ready for sing-along fun!

Enjoy these upbeat songs with your child as you travel...at bedtime...during playtime...any time! Every time you play this tape you'll help your child remember and apply important Bible truths!

These are the same songs you'll find in the *Pray & Play Bible for Young Children*— happy, encouraging songs your child will love!

● Each song is only about 45 seconds long—so they're quick to learn!

● Every song reinforces a *Pray & Play Bible* story!

● This is children's music even grown-ups like!

● BONUS: Chadder the Chipmunk—a cuddly puppet character your child probably already knows—quickly reviews all 14 *Pray & Play Bible* stories on this audiocassette...so children grow in faith every time they hear this tape!

Share these 37 bright, happy songs with your child!

ISBN 0-7644-3045-9

Four Read-Along Stories That Unfold Before Your Children's Eyes!

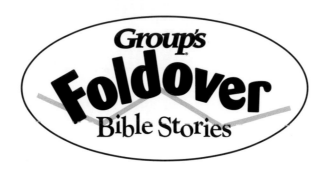

Treat your children to books that take storytelling to *new lengths*— a full 80 inches!

Each **Foldover Bible Story** invites your children to help solve a problem...

- *Do You See the Star?* follows a shepherd as he searches for a distant glow.
  ISBN 1-55945-617-5

- *Jesus, What's for Lunch?* considers a favorite Bible story from the viewpoint of a child who is way past lunch time.
  ISBN 1-55945-620-5

- In *Little Lamb, Where Did You Go?* children join a young shepherd in looking high and low for a lost lamb.
  ISBN 1-55945-618-3

- In *Noah, Noah, What'll We Do?* Noah needs help sorting out mixed-up animals.
  ISBN 1-55945-619-1

Lively, rhyming text and vivid illustrations hint at possible solutions, so even your youngest children will offer suggestions as the story unfolds. But not until the very last panel is everything clear!

Bonus "For Extra Fun" pages give you new craft and snack ideas to explore and to help you celebrate these stories with your children!

Order all four **Foldover Bible Story** books *now* and delight children in Sunday school...children's church...preschool...at home...*anywhere* children love to snuggle up to a good story!

Order today from your local Christian bookstore, or write: Group Publishing, P.O. Box 485, Loveland, CO 80539.